BENJAMIN WEST

AND THE TASTE OF HIS TIMES

Benjamin West. Self-Portrait, *ca.* 1770.

National Gallery of Art, Washington, D. C. (Mellon Collection)

BENJAMIN WEST

AND THE TASTE OF HIS TIMES

GROSE EVANS

Carbondale

SOUTHERN ILLINOIS UNIVERSITY PRESS

MCMLIX

ACKNOWLEDGMENTS

I would like to express my gratitude to the many collectors and museums who have kindly furnished information and photographs of works by Benjamin West. The staff of the Frick Art Reference Library has been especially helpful in permitting me to study their files on West's paintings. I have been encouraged in this study by Professor Richard Howland and guided by the advice of Professor Christopher Gray, both of Johns Hopkins University. Suggestions have also been received from Professor E. R. Wasserman of that faculty; from Miss Margaret Whinney of the Courtauld Institution, London; from Mr. Anthony Blunt, Keeper of the Queen's Pictures; from Professor Helmut von Erffa; and from James Thomas Flexner.

I would like to remember also the kindness of Mr. Charles Stotler of the National Gallery of Art who has been indefatigable in securing books, that of my brother, Professor G. Blakemore Evans, and that of my wife, all of whom have helped materially.

G. E.

TABLE OF CONTENTS

————— ✳ —————

LIST OF ILLUSTRATIONS

———————— ✳ ————————

BENJAMIN WEST

AND THE TASTE OF HIS TIMES

INTRODUCTION

———————— ✿ ————————

THE very colorful story of Benjamin West's rise from a humble inn-keeper's son in Pennsylvania to the position of President of the Royal Academy in London has been often told.[1] Recently his early pictures painted in America have been carefully analyzed to show what influences determined his first works,[2] and his youthful associations with cultured men have been investigated.[3] In this way considerable interest has been focused on West's early phase but, surprisingly, most of the figure compositions he painted in England, upon which his former reputation rested, remain unpublished and undiscussed.

The neglect of West's mature paintings is remarkable because he was a leader in forming European and American taste after his first success in London, 1766, until his death in 1820. During this time he exerted a very wide influence, helping to form the Royal Academy and extending generous aid to many American artists. Indeed, almost every American painter who reached maturity in these years felt West's influence to some degree.[4] He won the warm admiration of his students, and his art was frequently praised by men of taste.[5]

3

To understand the enthusiastic approval West's pictures won, the eighteenth-century criteria of judgment must be recalled. This study undertakes to revive the artistic aims of West's age, and to examine his mature figure compositions in the light of eighteenth-century expectations.

INTRODUCTION TO WEST'S MATURE STYLISTIC DEVELOPMENT

Before describing the phases through which West's painting developed in England, it is desirable to see his evolution in over-all perspective and to suggest some convenient terms for the different aspects of his style. In the past, the general terms Neoclassical and Romantic have been applied to his pictures. In fact, he has been cited as an innovator of Neoclassicism,[6] and a prophet of Romanticism,[7] but through general usage these terms have been appropriated to other artists at later dates. David is the Neoclassicist par excellence, and Delacroix, Turner, Constable, and a host of others are considered the Romantics. This study will not be concerned with either Neoclassicism or Romanticism. The aim is to trace West's development and find the reasons for his several changes of style. Clearly it would be pointless to seek an explanation for his art by defining it in terms descriptive of independent and later movements, even though West did anticipate certain aspects of them. For this reason the designations Neoclassical and Romantic will not be used to indicate West's styles, but more purely descriptive terms, suggested by his different types of painting, will be adopted.

The first of these descriptive terms is the "Stately Mode," and it will apply to the many pictures West painted in which the figures reflect that "sedate grandure" Wincklemann had extolled in ancient sculpture. An example of this manner is West's "Agrippina Landing at Brundisium" (Pl. 1) wherein the central group brings antique sculpture strongly to mind (cf. relief from the "Ara Pacis," Pl. 2). In the Stately Mode the figures appear sculpturesquely solid, reserved in their actions, and never expressive of strong emotions in their faces.

Quite distinct from this predominantly early manner is a second style which can be illustrated by "The Angel of the Lord Announcing the Resurrection" (Pl. 3). It is different from the previous example in mood, in composition, and in figure treatment. A greater emotional excitement is conveyed by the swirling drapery and the twisting, agitated figures. Light and shadow alternate here in small, broken areas to heighten the effect of restless motion. The figures are no longer ranged across the foreground, but lead back into depth; their forms do not recall ancient sculpture, because they are less insistently modeled than the earlier ones. This style will be called the "Dread Manner," for in it West obeyed the dictates of the "terrible sublime," a popular concept in eighteenth-century England.

Finally, a third phase will be called the "Pathetic Style." This term has been selected to describe those pictures in which figures become agents who stir the spectator's sentiments by an overt display of their own emotional states. While all painting is to some extent "pathetic" in the eighteenth-century sense, i.e., emotionally stimulating, the word seems particularly applicable to West's late works. In such paintings as "Christ Healing the Sick" (Pl. 4) he has made so strong a point of trying to arouse sympathies by showing his figures under varying emotional strains, that "pathetic" becomes an apt label for this style.

To some extent the three phases, the Stately, the Dread, and the

Pathetic, play throughout West's career. For instance, "The Death of General Wolfe" (Pl. 5), painted in 1769,[8] is compatible with the Stately Mode in its poised, well-modeled figures, and in its traditional Grand Manner, yet its emotional overtones ally it with the Pathetic Style. Or again, West painted "Saul and the Witch of Endor" (Pl. 6) in 1777, at a time when most of his work was in the Stately Mode, but it meets the qualifications of the Dread Manner with its sense of excitement and terror. His most "dread" picture, the final version of "Death on the Pale Horse" (Pl. 45), was done at a time when most of his pictures were "pathetic." But these instances are exceptional, and, generally speaking, West evolved from the Stately, through the Dread, to the Pathetic style.

Approximate periods may be assigned in which each of these manners predominated in West's work. The first twenty years of his English career (1763–83) were largely devoted to the Stately Mode, the Dread Manner preoccupied him for about the next twenty-two years (1783–1805), and roughly the last fifteen years were given to the Pathetic Style. These periods must be understood as indicative only of West's major interests during these times. They do not imply that his style changed precisely in certain years without preparatory, transitional works, nor that he could not paint a Stately, Dread, or Pathetic picture at any time in his development. These stylistic names indicate distinct esthetic aims, which engaged West's interest, broadly speaking, one after another. The realization that they do form a sequence of development is essential for understanding West's artistic achievement. If these major styles could not be resolved into chronological sequence, if West had constantly varied his styles throughout his life, the conclusion would have to be drawn that the particular subject he was painting dictated the treatment or determined the style. Such was undoubtedly the case in some instances, especially in an exceptional picture like "The Death of General Wolfe," where the requirements of the subject led West beyond the effects usual in his current paintings. Also in transitional phases of his development, the subject matter exerted influences tending to alter his style. For example, a picture like "The Raising of Lazarus" (Pl. 8) shows some of the restraint of the Stately Mode, but the subject of Christ's miracle has led West to concentrate a greater feeling of excitement and animation in the figures than is compatible with the esthetic aims of the Stately Mode. The picture is not yet in the Dread Manner, but the theme has determined a move in that direction. However, despite exceptional and transitional works, it is possible to say that West's esthetic aims usually determined not only his style, but even his choice of subjects. When his artistic aims had matured in his mind, his subjects were selected to support them. Consequently, in the following chapters on West's three major phases, his choice of themes will be considered along with the characteristics of his styles, because both were largely determined by the changing esthetic ideals guiding his development.

CHAPTER ONE

BACKGROUND FOR WEST'S
HISTORY PAINTING

————————— ✱ —————————

IN 1766, three years after Benjamin West had settled in London, he painted "Pylades and Orestes" (Pl. 9), and exhibited it in his studio. It was sensationally successful. "His house was soon filled with visitors from all quarters to see it; and those amongst the highest rank, who were not able to come to his house to satisfy their curiosity, desired his permission to have it sent to them; nor did they fail, every time it was returned to him, to accompany it with compliments of the highest commendation on its great merits."[1]

West's picture did more than catch the popular fancy, for it embodied cultural ideals which had been developing in England for many years. The success of his picture recalls the similar triumph enjoyed by Anton Raphael Mengs five years earlier when his "Parnassus" (Pl. 14) was completed in Rome.[2] A few years later, in 1785, Jacques-Louis David also won widespread satisfaction by his "Oath of the Horatii."[3] In all of these cases the artists had produced pictures which more than fulfilled the expectations of their contemporaries. Behind the general enthusiasm for "Pylades and Orestes" lay the eighteenth-

9

century Englishman's longing for a share in the great classical tradition of art.

In both theme and execution "Pylades and Orestes" was found thoroughly acceptable. It illustrates the moment in Euripides' *Iphigenia in Taurica* when Orestes and his friend Pylades have been captured by the Tauric barbarians, and are brought before Iphigenia. She is to prepare them for sacrifice to Diana, but after a short conversation, Orestes recognizes Iphigenia as his sister, whom he had believed dead for many years. She also had thought Orestes dead, so a joyful reunion takes place, and eventually they escape with Pylades from the barbarians. It is an appealing, sentimental episode.

While the subject was a pleasant one, the picture owed its high success to the particular way West painted the figures. His contemporaries would have recognized affinities between these painted forms and the admired marble statues of ancient Rome. They would have felt West's debt to Raphael's type of composition, even though perhaps they would not have guessed his actual sources.[4] Both the Antique and Raphael were held in highest esteem at this time, and the remarkable popularity of "Pylades and Orestes" must be understood as a happy coincidence between West's training and a well established British taste for art in the classical vein. Therefore, before West's first manner of painting is studied, his own background must be briefly noticed, and an effort must be made to reconstruct the taste of his times which he satisfied so well.

TRAINING

Benjamin West was born on October 10, 1738, in Springfield Township, Pennsylvania. His father kept an inn which still stands on the campus of Swarthmore College. His early years were spent in a Quaker community where paintings were rarely seen, but his own first efforts in drawing were encouraged by his family. At the age of eight he received the gift of a paint box and six engravings by "Grevling" from a Pennsylvania merchant.[5] Soon he was copying figures from the prints, recombining them to form new pictures. It is amusing to find that his earliest figure compositions were composed in this eclectic way, for he continued the method in his mature pictures.

When West was nine years old, his knowledge of artistic tradition was enlarged by a trip to Philadelphia. Here he might have seen a few original pictures by European painters, particularly in the collection of Governor Hamilton,[6] and he was introduced to an itinerant English artist, William Williams, who gave him his first real instruction. Williams painted portraits and groups in garden settings in the vein of Highmore, but with less skill.[7] Williams probably offered West a great deal of help in the technical handling of paint, and he introduced West to European academic theories of art by lending him two treatises on art. The books were Charles du Fresnoy's *De Arte Graphica*, probably Dryden's translation, and an essay by Jonathan Richardson, the English painter and connoisseur.[8]

West's education was supervised by the provost of the college at Philadelphia, who stressed the classics, especially the ancient myths and classical history, since these would serve West for subject matter in his art. His early training in painting can hardly have been very extensive because Philadelphia had few resident artists, and there was no local school of painting as in Boston and New York. James Claypoole was a Philadelphia painter, born in 1720, and recorded as active there until about 1750. He was the uncle and teacher of Matthew

Pratt, who became West's friend and later his pupil in London. Probably Claypoole influenced West's early work, and it is unfortunate that no work by him has been identified.[9] Whether he could have instructed West in figure composition is doubtful, but not impossible, because Philadelphians had great pride in elaborately painted signboards which demanded some knowledge of the figure-painter's skill. William Dunlap described some of these shop signs which Pratt later painted, and perhaps Claypoole and West had done their share of signs as well.[10]

West's early paintings were largely portraits which reveal his study of pictures available in Philadelphia. He could have seen portraits by Gustavus Hesselius (1682–1755), Robert Feke (*ca.* 1705–*ca.* 1750), John Hesselius (1728–78), and John Wollaston (active 1749–67).[11] The most lasting impression upon West was made by Wollaston, an Englishman, who came to New York in 1749, and was active in the southern states and Pennsylvania between 1758 and 1767.[12] His style was highly artificial, derived from the hard manner of Gottfried Kneller (1646–1723), the London favorite. Wollaston formalized his subjects' faces to such an extent that they all look astonishingly alike, yet he enjoyed wide popularity, which may have determined West to imitate his style. West's "Elizabeth Peel" (Pl. 12) shows Wollaston's treatment of features; particularly characteristic are the "almond eyes," but the drapery is less sophisticated than Wollaston's, for he would never have resolved the folds into so obviously rhythmic a pattern.

West is believed to have been active in Philadelphia between 1756 and 1760.[13] Some months of the latter year were spent in New York City, where West painted portraits and saved his money for a trip to Italy. If he were to become a "history painter" such a trip was necessary, because no adequate training was available in America. One of his earliest history pieces is "The Death of Socrates" (Pl. 13), painted for the wealthy gunsmith William Henry, of Lancaster, Pennsylvania.[14] It reveals the serious deficiencies in West's knowledge of the accepted conventions for figure proportions, anatomy, and drapery treatment, although it is not without merits as an academic composition, and shows a certain aptitude for catching dramatic gestures and facial expressions. Clearly, if West were to grow beyond the provincial quality of this work, the Italian trip was a necessity. So in 1760 he sailed to Italy, and the three years he spent there were the most formative of his life. From his Italian studies he emerged a remarkably accomplished artist.

EXPERIENCES IN ITALY

On July 10, 1760, West was hardly more than installed in his Roman lodgings before a wealthy English dilettante Mr. Robinson, afterwards Lord Grantham, came to see him.[15] Robinson's curiosity had been roused when he heard of this young colonial, the first from the wilds of the New World to come seeking artistic education in Rome. A friendship began which was of great value to West, because Robinson was able to introduce him at once into circles where art and antiquity were the constant topics of conversation. Together they visited the many distinguished collections of ancient marbles which Rome offered. The Capitoline Museum had been enlarged by the Pope in 1734, and was open to the public. Visitors could gain admission to the Vatican galleries where acquisitions had accumulated since the Renaissance. Great private collections had been formed during the seventeenth century in many Roman palaces: the Adobrandini, Ludovisi, Borghese, Farnese, Giustiniani, Pamfili, and many more.[16] All of these might be seen if the visitor knew a prominent dilettante or scholar, who would introduce and guide him. Through his friend Robinson, West was able to tour these collections, and meet Cardinal Albani. Although blind, this churchman was considered to be among the leading authorities on ancient art, and was completing his collection in the Villa Albani. West must have seen it, because he met Anton Raphael Mengs at the Cardinal's villa.[17]

Through Robinson, West also met Gavin Hamilton, an English painter, who had come to Rome when young and developed a passion for antiques. Hamilton had excavated in the Roman Campagna, and frequently supplied English collectors with ancient statues. Both Hamilton and Mengs had caught the new enthusiasm for antiquity which was fostered by Johann Winckelmann, the leading scholar of ancient art.[18] West must have acquired a similar reverence for the antique by association with these two painters, because he was soon to incorporate Winckelmann's theories in his own pictures.

Winckelmann was a German antiquarian who came to Rome in 1755. Born in 1717, this son of a Brandenburg cobbler had studied theology at Halle, and held various teaching posts. His study of classical literature led him to Rome to seek out the actual remains of the ancients, and led him further to Herculaneum, Pompeii, and Paestum. His preoccupation with these southern sites coincided with the period of West's visit to Italy, and explains why West never met him in Rome.[19] A few years earlier, when Winckelmann was in Rome, he was a well known figure, often earning his living as a guide for the wealthy tourists. He was extremely popular with them because he combined enthusiasm with considerable scholarship, and so he could enliven ancient art with his knowledge of classical life, habits, and beliefs. His many published writings show the popularity of his method.[20] Just before his arrival in Rome he published *Gedanken über die Nachahmung der griechischen Werke in Malerie und Bildhauerkunst* (Dresden, 1755), containing the ideas which became current while West was in Rome. Winckelmann's central doctrine was not new: "there is but one way for the moderns to become great, and perhaps unequaled; I mean by imitating the ancients."[21] While this point was generally acknowledged in seventeenth-century art theory, Winckelmann's taste indicated certain aspects of ancient art as superior to others. In the varied range of style in antique works, Winckelmann offered guidance, indicating which styles were most worthy of imitation. He preached an esthetic of emotional restraint, saying, "The last and most eminent characteristic of the Greek works is a noble simplicity and sedate grandeur in Gesture and Expression."[22] Such a description conjures before a modern mind the Greek art of the fifth and fourth centuries B.C., but it must be remembered that Winckelmann knew very few works of that period. In reality he was speaking about his favorites, the "Apollo Belvedere," the "Venus de' Medici," and curiously enough about the far from restrained "Laocoon" group. He could not resist admiring the "Laocoon," and mentioned the "pangs piercing every muscle, every laboring nerve; pangs which we almost feel ourselves," but he concluded, "these however, I say, exert not themselves with violence either in the face or gesture."[23] "Laocoon" was valued for its relative restraint in view of the possible violence which its theme might have occasioned. Other ancient statues with little emotional expression, whose faces and gestures were devoid of feeling, were reconcilable in

15

this way with the "Laocoon." All were praised for expressing an ideal, or universal, aspect of nature. Winckelmann demanded that a work should fulfill his imaginative expectation of the hero or god represented. It was for this reason that the "Apollo Belvedere" and the "Venus de' Medici" might become canons of perfection; not that they embodied any secret of perfect proportion or formal beauty, but because they convincingly incarnated the idea of godhood. They were superb pieces of illustration, and as such they supported the conviction of the time that sculpture, painting, and poetry were sister arts, capable of illustrating the godlike, heroic order of nature which obsessed the cultured minds of the period. It was a vigorous, imaginative ideal claiming that ethical and physical perfection should pervade all the forms an artist created.

The contemporary artist who best reflected Winckelmann's ideals was Anton Mengs. Winckelmann said that beside Mengs's "Parnassus" (Pl. 14) Guido Reni's famous "Aurora" seemed to be only the product of common, mortal hands. Mengs, he thought, had even surpassed Raphael, for "all the beauties which the ancients captured in their works . . . are to be found in the immortal masterpieces of Anton Raphael Mengs."[24]

The "Parnassus" was finished between 1760 and 1761, and West would have seen it when he met Mengs in the Villa Albani, where the picture was being painted. It became the talk of the town, winning general approval, and West must have studied it carefully since his own early figure compositions resemble it in many respects.

Mengs, who became the most fashionable painter in Rome, had come from Bohemia at the age of thirteen in 1741. His teacher was Benefiale, master also of Revett, and one of the first to turn away from the Baroque classicism of Bernini, Algardi, and Cortona. Benefiale had found too much "common nature" in the work of these High Baroque masters, and he preached a stricter imitation of classical sculpture. His enthusiasm for the ancients had kindled a similar love of the Antique in his pupil, Pompeo Batoni, whom West saw painting on one occasion.[25] Batoni was a brilliant executant of paintings, but his style remained essentially Baroque. Mengs, twenty years younger than he, broke more radically with the existing traditions to follow a taste akin to Winckelmann's. Yet even in Mengs's work a strong heritage from the earlier century remained, a kinship especially with previous classicism, which will be seen if his "Parnassus" is compared with Domenichino's "Hunt of Diana" (Pl. 15). In both pictures the figure of the god is the compositional center, standing silhouetted against a dark mass of foliage. In both, the subservient figures balance either side of the foreground. The comparison will show, however, that Mengs based his figures more directly upon ancient statues than did Domenichino. His Apollo's slender proportions recall the "Apollo Belvedere," while its pose could have been derived from the many imitations of Praxitelian figures found on Greco-Roman sarcophagi. But the Antique alone was not enough for Mengs. He sweetened and sentimentalized his figures, because of an admiration for Raphael and Correggio. In fact, as a practical painter, Mengs had to draw from sources other than antiquity. The ancient statues and reliefs would not supply acceptable examples of pictorial composition, and there was little ancient painting which might be consulted. Winckelmann acknowledged that what was left of classical painting was poor, and believed that the Renaissance Italians had outstripped the ancients in some branches of painting, especially in perspective.[26] So Mengs's dependence upon recent painting traditions was inescapable. He attempted to merge antiquity and the Renaissance into a unified style, arguing, "I conclude from all that I have said, that the Painter who would wish to obtain a good, or be it the best Taste, ought to learn from the ancients the *Taste of Beauty*, from Raphael the *Taste of Expression*, from Correggio that of *Pleasing, and of Harmony*, and from Titian that of *Truth and of Colouring*."[27]

This eclectic program, which Mengs advocated, was almost identical with that blend of the Antique, Raphael, Correggio, and Titian which had been favored by the Bolognese Academy 150 years earlier.[28] Hence it is not remarkable to find the "Parnassus" resembling the style of Domenichino, who was trained in Bologna, and later in Rome by Annibale Carracci, one of the founders of the Bolognese Baroque style. Indeed, the current popularity of Bolognese pictures may have led Mengs into his eclecticism. Though Winckelmann found Annibale's Farnese Gallery unpleasing, its decoration was quite different from the Bolognese style of altarpiece and easel picture, both of which were widely admired. Domenichino's "Last Communion of St. Jerome," in the Vatican, was thought second only to Raphael's "Transfiguration," and Ludovico Carracci's huge "Transfiguration," in the Bologna Gallery (Pl. 40), with figures twice the size of life, was another favorite of the time.[29]

There is no indication that West became intimate with Mengs, but once when Robinson showed Mengs a portrait by West, which was acknowledged to be better in coloring than Mengs's own work, the master offered the young artist some advice: " 'You have already, sir,' said he, 'the mechanical part of your art: what I would, therefore, recommend to you, is to see and examine everything deserving of your attention here, and after making a few drawings of about half a dozen of the best statues, go to Florence, and observe what has been done for Art in the collections there. Then proceed to Bologna, and study the works of the Carracci; afterwards visit Parma, and examine, attentively, the pictures of Correggio; and then go to Venice, and view the productions of Tintoretti, Titian, and Paul Veronese. When you have made this tour, come back to Rome, and paint an historical composition to be exhibited to the Roman public; and the opinion which will then be formed of your talents should determine the line of our profession which you ought to follow.' "[30]

Mengs's suggestions probably fitted well with West's own plans, because he hoped to see as much of Italian art as possible. But before he could set out on his travels, he suffered a serious setback: a nervous illness and an injured leg. These ailments confined him to his rooms for eight months. He was in Leghorne for a while, but later was able to move to Florence, the first town on Mengs's itinerary. While there, he passed the time drawing and painting in his bed, and enjoyed visits from various of the British nobility, so that his time was not wasted in view of his later career in England. When he recovered, he set out to see the cities Mengs had suggested, and with him went a Dr. Matthews, "out of all comparison, the best practical antiquary, perhaps, then in that country."[31] Thus West's interest in the Antique was kept amply alive.

West saw the collections in Florence, Bologna, Venice, and Parma, as recommended, and added Genoa, Turin, and Lucca to his travels. While in Parma he copied a "St. Jerome" by Correggio, and was made an honorary member of the academy there. Finally, he returned to Rome and painted two pictures which won the acclaim of the Roman critics.[32] These paintings are lost today, and indeed very little remains from West's studies in Italy.[33] Of figure paintings, done in his three years there, only a few copies after old masters have been found. One of these will suffice for examination, the "Christ on the Mount of Olives" (Pl. 18). Formerly this was considered an original composition, but comparison with Tiepolo's "Agony in the Garden" (Pl. 17), Civic Museum, Würzburg, proves it to be a copy.[34] Since he has even copied the light, fluent brush work of Tiepolo's style, his picture must have been done from the original, which might have been in Venice when he studied there.

Such copies as this can tell us little of West's progress. It will be more profitable to examine a slightly later painting in relation to West's study in Italy in order to see how completely his trip formed his style. His "Rinaldo and Armida" (Pl. 16), painted a few years after leaving Rome, will serve to show his sympathy with Mengs's ideals. The figures are in the slender proportions Mengs had used in his "Parnassus" (Pl. 14). Armida is shown in a profile view in conformity with figures in ancient reliefs. The figures and faces have been sweetened and modeled in a way that brings to mind Mengs's favorite, Correggio, and the deep shadows of the wooded background remind one of Titian's use of light and shade. In all, it is a proficient picture in the approved eclectic style then current in Rome. If it is compared with West's earlier "Death of Socrates" (Pl. 13), painted before his trip to Italy, it will demonstrate that he had achieved the cultured taste he sought.

After West won critical commendation in Rome, he started the return journey to America. He saw a little of France, which he did not like, and then he stopped in London. Here he spent the rest of his life, for as a colonial Englishman he must have realized that there was little need for his art in America, and that he should seek laurels in the heart of the British Empire.

CAREER IN ENGLAND

When West settled in London on August 20, 1763, he received generous encouragement from all to whom he brought letters of introduction. He was taken to see many private collections, including those at Storehead, Fonthill, Wilton House, and Longford Castle, as well as the public collections at Hampton Court, Blenheim, and Oxford.[35] He soon knew many artists, especially Sir Joshua Reynolds and Richard Wilson. After two years of painting in London he felt sufficiently self-assured to have Elizabeth Shewell, a boyhood sweetheart, brought from Philadelphia to become his wife. At about the same time Dr. Drummond, Archbishop of York, became an especial admirer of West's figure pieces, and commissioned "Agrippina Landing at Brundisium" (Pl. 1), which was shown to George III. The king was much impressed and ordered West to paint "The Departure of Regulus" (Pl. 19).

A friendship developed between the king and West, which remained firm even though West was quite outspoken in his sympathy with the Americans during the Revolution. In 1772 West became the royal painter of history pieces, and continued to enjoy the king's patronage for about thirty years. Assurance of financial support from the Crown made it possible for West to continue painting figure compositions instead of having to earn his living by portrait painting. The king's aid also allowed West freedom to become an innovator of artistic styles during his mature development.

21

Because of his intimacy with the king, West was very influential in founding the Royal Academy in 1768. Later he succeeded Reynolds as its president in 1792, and occupied this post, except for a brief retirement in 1805, until his death in 1820.[36] His election as President of the Royal Academy was curious, for he was not a man of broad cultural attainments. Though he was introduced into the distinguished circle of Reynolds, Samuel Johnson, Oliver Goldsmith, and Edmund Burke, there is no indication that he became intimate with any of these men. He lacked their polish and education—even his grammar and speech were marked by colonial eccentricities—because his training had been pointed only towards the career of painter.[37] In this respect, it is amusing to cite the character Mrs. West gave of her famous husband to the diarist, Joseph Farington: "Mrs. West told me that in the 40 years she had been married to Mr. West she had never but once seen him intoxicated: & never seen him in a passion.—She said that He was so devoted to drawing while a child, and a youth, that every other part of education was neglected."[38]

West was indeed simply a painter, and had acquired only enough culture to allow him to practice in the elegant manner of his time. To be sure, this style demanded considerable education; he had to know ancient art and literature, history, and Italian painting and art theory. He needed a working knowledge of anatomy and perspective. As an aid in acquiring some of this necessary background, West began to form a collection of pictures and of prints after famous works. In time his collections became very extensive, and offered him an intimate understanding of the accepted European masters' styles.[39] Such knowledge was essential to his eclectic system of composing, and it rounded out his artistic education.

ENGLISH EIGHTEENTH-CENTURY CLASSICISM

In the course of the eighteenth century England made great advances, spreading her Empire, increasing her foreign trade, and reaping the benefits of the Industrial Revolution, which made her home industries far more productive. Many families, achieving wealth, sought to improve themselves by also acquiring the sophistication of European culture. Early in the century the Grand Tour, a cultural pilgrimage to Italy, was considered essential to complete an education. These tours centered chiefly in Rome, since from the High Renaissance Rome had assumed leadership in determining European taste. Rome alone could offer the artistic authority of two great, interrelated cultures, antiquity and the Renaissance. A single classical tradition, uniting the art of Imperial Rome with that of Raphael and Michelangelo, brought the city an extraordinary cultural distinction. Only in Rome could an artist or dilettante study extensively both the ancient statues and Renaissance paintings acknowledged in West's time as the fountainhead from which future art should spring. Other classical sites, notably Herculaneum and Pompeii,[40] contained far more remains showing intimately the life of the ancients, but these towns did not replace Rome as the center of antiquarian interest. The spoils excavated at Herculaneum were jealously guarded in the royal palace at Portici, which was difficult of access, and government restrictions prevented even sketching among the ruins of Pompeii until after 1800. Consequently, publication of the finds was meager, and Rome retained her position of leadership in disseminating classical taste until the nineteenth century.[41] Rome's position had also been strengthened by the seventeenth-century worship of her past accomplishment; criteria of esthetic judgment had been found in her ancient monuments, and the seal of approval set upon those Renaissance and Baroque artists who drew most strongly upon them.[42] This attitude was recorded in many art treatises, and through their wide dispersion, it became prevalent and dominant throughout Europe, establishing classicism in all academies, and drawing artists to Rome.

By 1760, when West visited Rome, the city was filled with lively discussion about the art of antiquity. The English gentlemen on their Grand Tours were beginning to buy as much ancient sculpture as they could, and this busy traffic in antiques sharpened the existing interest in them. When the Italians found their visitors so keen to collect, the "restoration" of fragments into handsome, complete figures became a thriving trade, carried on surreptitiously in the Colosseum. However, many excellent examples were secured by English collectors, especially from the old, impoverished Italian families.

After 1750, when England entered upon its heyday of dilettantism, London became second only to Rome itself as a museum of Greek and Roman antiquities.[43] Dr. Richard Mead, the most famous physician of the early eighteenth century, visiting Italy in 1795, returned with several marble statues as well as a large collection of coins and small bronze statuettes. The scholar Conyers Middleton also had many souvenirs from his Italian trip in 1724, including small bronzes, lamps, and sacrificial or culinary utensils. Dr. Hans Sloane, physician of George I, filled his Chelsea house with thirty-two thousand antiquities, which in 1753 he gave to the nation as the basis of the British Museum classical department. Besides such London collections, the great country houses were richly decorated with ancient sculpture. Thomas Herbert, eighth Earl of Pembroke, formed the Wilton collection before

1732. He bought many of the pieces formerly in the great Arundel collection, and added to this over 360 antique sculptures from Cardinal Mazarin's gallery. He also purchased many items from the Guistiniani family in Rome. The large Palladian mansions, Chiswick, Holkham Hall, and Castle Howard all had extensive collections, and Egremont's Petworth Castle contained one of England's largest.

The passion for collecting ancient statuary continued throughout the century. The most notable later collector was Charles Townley, who amassed a very impressive group of marbles between 1765 and 1772. He installed the works in his mansion, which became one of the sights of London. In quality, this collection was outdone by that of the first Marquis of Lansdowne, who bought from Gavin Hamilton after his excavations of 1770–80. An interest in ancient small bronzes was sustained by Richard Payne Knight, the connoisseur and guiding spirit of the Dilettanti Society, who built up a fine collection after 1785. He opposed the purchase of the Elgin marbles from the Parthenon, which was the last and most notable collection of this period. Elgin's fragments arrived in London in 1806, and were at last purchased by the government in 1816. They arrived too late to determine English classicism, but they re-enforced this taste, and strengthened the growing interest in Greece. West saw and copied the Elgin marbles in 1809, and, with Fuseli and B. R. Haydon, distinguished himself by defending them against Knight's prejudice.[44]

Besides this remarkable importation of classical statues to England, the many books with illustrations of ancient art should be remembered as influential in forming Britain's classicism. Volumes of engravings were cheaper and more easily portable than the statues themselves. Their quantity and popularity were attested by Horace Walpole, who wrote that hardly an important Roman collection existed without its illustrated catalogue.[45] In addition to the Roman books, a few were available on Greek remains.[46] In fact, the Parthenon sculptures were first introduced to England by the plates in Stuart and Revett, *Antiquities of Athens*, vol. II (1787), nearly twenty years before the marbles themselves arrived. Such engravings were an important aid to artists, eager to increase their familiarity with ancient art, and their influence was extensive. Added to these books of reproductions were the scholarly publications of Winckelmann, which brought to England much of the new enthusiasm for ancient works, so that many in England could share something of the feeling which had fired West's imagination in Rome. Winckelmann's particular opinions, however, should not be too greatly stressed. His real function was to enliven an existing admiration for the classical tradition. He was but one of many exponents of classicizing idealism whose theories reached England, and the others must be mentioned next.

CONTINENTAL INFLUENCES ON ENGLISH ART THEORY

In the seventeenth century England had absorbed cultural ideals from Italy and from France, where the Italian theories were echoed. The popularity of these schools was due undoubtedly to the power of the pen as much as the appeal of the brush, for both Italy and France produced a weighty literature on art. Treatises were written in the Italian and French academies to formulate prevalent judgment on art, and these tracts were sought by Englishmen, entering upon a period of prosperity and turning to the arts as patrons, investors, and connoisseurs. Soon, in answer to their cultural needs, many translations of the European academic treatises were published in England. Moreover, original English treatises also began to appear, their ideas clearly derived from the European ones. These many books embodied essentially one theory of art, which will be discussed in the next chapter in connection with West's first mature style, but they contained different emphases. Several authors, Fréart de Chambray, Pierre Monier, George Turnbull, and others, shared Winckelmann's views on the supremacy of ancient art.[47] Classical art from the time of Phidias to about the end of the second century A.D. was held by these to have been man's supreme artistic achievement. While others praised ancient art, their main emphasis was placed less upon imitation of antiques than upon the creation of an art equally idealistic. Franciscus Junius, Giovanni Bellori, Charles du Fresnoy, Ludovico Dolce, and the Englishmen Jonathan Richardson and Joshua Reynolds were convinced that modern art should parallel, not imitate, the ancient style.[48]

During the eighteenth century little conflict was felt between the assertions that art must embody ideal nature, and that it should express passions and sentiments. At first thought, these two aims—towards beauty and towards expression—seem mutually exclusive, but they were held in harmony because both beauty and expression were to serve man's moral improvement. The current ethical aim of art was a common denominator that unified artistic aims which later fell into conflict. Expression was the truthful portrayal of elevating emotions, and beauty, too, had power to elevate the observer. While sustaining the theory that art should embody beauty, Giovanni Lomazzo, Charles Le Brun, André Félibien, Anthony, third Earl of Shaftesbury, and Benjamin Ralph primarily emphasized expressiveness.[49]

At the close of the seventeenth century, tendencies to accept genre and landscape as well as historical subjects became current in the French Academy. Rich coloring, as well as precise drawing, and imagination and feeling, as well as reason, were given new importance in esthetic consideration, marking a liberalization of the earlier classicists' views. Roger de Piles was the leading exponent of these new attitudes, and his *Abrégé de la Vie des Peintres* was translated into English in 1706. His famous *Balance des Peintres* was also made available to the English reader before the mid-century.[50]

Besides the authors mentioned here there were many others of less importance who presented synthesized opinions based on the views expressed by the leading classicists. An early, amusing book was William Aglionby's *Painting Illustrated in Three Dialogues* (London, 1686), wherein a well informed traveler airs his views on ancient art and on the approved Italian "moderns" for the benefit of an eager friend, intent upon acquiring culture. William Hayley, Blake's patron, and Sir Martin Archer Shee sustained the traditional classicist's standards throughout the century, though subjecting them to sentimentality.[51]

While the views of the authors cited here might vary slightly, there is remarkable general agreement in most of their thought. This body of belief will be analyzed in the next chapter as a background for West's first style of painting in England.

CHAPTER TWO

THE STATELY MODE

————————✳————————

BEFORE the pictures which West painted first in England can be approached with understanding, the academic theory guiding both his practice and his patron's taste must be reviewed.

CLASSICIZING AIMS AND THEORY OF ART

The seventeenth- and eighteenth-century treatises listed in the preceding chapter supplied a theoretical basis for English classicism in the fine arts. Since West echoed these writings in his Discourses before the Royal Academy, it is possible here to summarize both the classicizing aims of art and West's own artistic views.[1]

According to the classicist's point of view, art gave insight into the ideal realm of perfect goodness, truth, and beauty, and so afforded moral instruction, which was considered both pleasant and improving. Du Fresnoy recommended the "choice of a Subject beautiful and noble; which being of it self capable of all the Charms and Graces, that Colours, and the Elegance of Design can possibly give, shall afterwards afford . . . somewhat to the Sight, which is excellent, judicious, and ingenious; and at the same time proper to instruct, and to enlighten the Understanding."[2] Instructing and pleasing were nearly synonymous in classicizing theory, for the pleasures of sense were considered subservient to the pleasures of the mind,[3] and were only valued as they contributed towards knowledge of ethical and physical perfection, which was believed the ultimate satisfaction.

Art gave its pleasure, as Aristotle had said, by satisfying certain reasonable "instincts" for harmony and for imitation. Harmony presided over the sensuous pleasures derived from line, form, and color; its principle was proportion, or the golden mean.[4] Imitation meant to follow the actions of others, but in painting, though it lent a sanction to eclecticism, it meant basically the imitation of various aspects of nature.[5] In this latter sense, imitation was recognized as a fundamental explanation of art's appeal, because it was thought pleasurable to compare a copy with a remembered original, to derive pleasure from recognition. By extension, the imitation of a noble deed and of ideal beauty became the chief aim of art, since in heroic action and in perfect physical form man could recognize his own potential ethical and corporeal perfection.[6] These perfections were assumed to be awaiting recognition in man's moral nature,[7] and so art became a means for man to complete himself, to fill out his deficiencies, and accomplish the Creator's original intention, passing beyond the state of imperfection.

How man's moral nature might be touched through imitation afforded the substance of the classicizing art treatises. The answers they offered can be discussed under several broad categories, suggested by certain rubrics of the system: noble theme, ideal beauty, character, expression, and decorum.

THE NOBLE THEME

The ethical nature of man might be stirred most readily by a story of heroism, self-sacrifice, or noble love; eternal truth and the triumph of true faith might be revealed in a religious miracle. Such subjects, drawn from ancient history, myths, and from Christian lore were commended as most proper for painting.[8] This insistence upon morally significant subject matter was forcibly expressed by West in a letter of 1809 to Charles Willson Peale: "Although I am friendly to portraying eminent men, I am not friendly to the indiscriminate waste of genius in portrait painting . . . the art of painting has powers to dignify man, by transmitting to posterity his noble actions, and his mental powers, to be viewed in those invaluable lessons of religion, love of country, and morality; such subjects are worthy of the pencil, they are worthy of being placed in view as the most instructive records to a rising generation."[9] Biblical, classical, and historical themes with moral content were the constant sources of West's painting. Through them he maintained the classicist's didactic purpose of art.

IDEAL BEAUTY

Du Fresnoy said, "The principal and most important part of Painting, is to find out, and thoroughly to understand what Nature has made most Beautiful, and most proper to this Art. . . ."[10] Like all the major tenets of academic art theory, this esthetic aim had its origin in Aristotle's ideas of the highest literary art, tragedy: "Since tragedy is a representation of men better than ourselves we must copy the good portrait-painters who, while rendering the distinctive form and making a likeness, yet paint people better than they are."[11] This passage not

31

only established the aim of the most serious kind of art, but demonstrated that a taste for idealization in painting had existed in antiquity. There were many stories which bore out this notion, tales of ancient painters and sculptors who had achieved ideal beauty in their works. Perhaps the one most often repeated told how Zeuxis had made his "Helen" by selecting the best parts of several fair models, and combining them together to form a perfect whole.[12] This process of selection from external nature would yield figures which might assume universality as ideal types,[13] because they represented a nature purified of eccentricities, accidental particularities, as well as moral deficiencies. They embodied nature as it ought to be, most universal and representative, because most perfect, and nearest the Creator's intention.

How was the artist to achieve this perfected nature in his figures? To assist him there were three practical recommendations: the study of proportion, the study of ancient art, and the study of certain approved "moderns."

Proportion was conceived as a measured relationship between all parts of the human figure. What these parts were, and how they should be measured by simple mathematical ratio (by the unit measure of one head's height, or the length of a face, a nose, etc.) were details carefully prescribed by seventeenth-century theorists.[14] West gave the same instruction in his Discourse of 1797, describing precisely the anatomical sections which were the "parts" of the figure, and recommending that all drawings be "geometrical," i.e., measured. He concluded, "I would advise you to make from the Apollo and the Venus a general measurement or standard for man and woman, taking the head and its features, as the part by which you measure the division of those figures."[15]

West's recourse to the "Apollo Belvedere" and the "Venus de' Medici" in order to establish ideal proportions indicates that he shared the general regard for ancient sculpture. Though these particular statues did not exactly conform to the strict requirements of proportion, they were allowed to be superior to its rules. They presented the surest and most practical guide to the revelation of ideal nature, and current taste had to be formed upon the "Taste and Manner of the Ancients."[16]

In addition to the classical examples, various modern schools and masters, in whose work the spirit of antiquity was preserved, might also be studied with profit. The following were generally recommended: *Approved Schools*: Roman, Venetian, Parmesan, Bolognese. *Approved Artists*: Raphael for Invention, Michelangelo for Design, Romano for Nobleness, Correggio for Light and Shadow, Titian for Coloring, Annibale Carracci, whose style combined all these aspects.[17]

The academicians' insistence that taste be formed by study of the ancient statues and of the classicizing moderns made eclecticism in practice inevitable. Borrowed figure poses and compositional devices became the commonplace vocabulary of seventeenth- and eighteenth-century painting. This eclecticism must be evaluated in the context of academic theory; it was clearly necessary for the preservation of Antique traditions, which had to be maintained as the fountainhead of perfect beauty. While modern esthetic opinion may regard such eclecticism as crippling to originality, the classicist himself must have considered it a solemn duty. Only by imitation of the classical style could nature be elevated to an ideal state.

But imitation did not mean simply copying; instead it meant adapting traditional forms to new purposes. Winckelmann asserted the difference when he wrote, "Copying we call the slavish crawling of the hand and eyes, after a certain model: whereas reasonable imitation just takes the hint, in order to work by itself. . . . Copying I call, moreover, the following of a certain form, without the least consciousness of one's being a blockhead."[18] Sir Joshua Reynolds also concerned himself with this difference in his twelfth Discourse. Copying, he thought, would be only slightly beneficial, but imitation was sanctioned by the example of Raphael, and he concluded, "A readiness in taking such hints, which escape the dull and ignorant, makes in my opinion no inconsiderable part of that faculty of the mind which is called Genius."[19] This favorable attitude towards imitation was fundamental to West's artistic practice, and throughout his life he adapted traditional motifs, figures, and compositional arrangements to new purposes in his pictures.

Once taste had been formed upon tradition, the artist was urged to turn to nature, "for she it is from whom Art derives her ultimate Perfection." However, the word nature in this context must be understood as implying that aspect of external nature towards which taste will direct the artist. "Nature" came to mean ideal nature. So Wincklemann understood it when he wrote, "Building on this ground, his hand and senses directed by the Greek rule of beauty, the modern artist goes on the surest way to the imitation of Nature."[20]

West sustained the theory of eclecticism throughout his life, and in his Discourses cited the schools and painters listed above as the origins from which good taste must be developed, and finally admonished the student to study nature.[21]

CHARACTER

Nature interpreted as universal forms was by no means fixed and rigid in its appearances.[22] There was not one ideal form of man, but many. Ideal types were conditioned by specific, known characteristics and by temporal, spatial, and psychological circumstances. All such aspects of life played a part in satisfying the expectations of reason. For example, Hercules shown overcoming Antaeus would have to be depicted as a physical type very different from that of Apollo riding in his chariot. Though their types were distinct, they were both ideal masculine figures. West expressed this classical theory in one of his Discourses to the Academy when he said of the Greeks, "To all their deities a fixed and appropriate character was given, from which it would have perhaps been profanity to depart. This character was the result of a careful consideration of the ideal beauty suitable to the respective attributes of the different deities."[23] The achievement of "appropriate character" was the aim West constantly set before the Academy students. In simpler terms, it means apt illustration of certain type-characters. West's phrase echoes Aristotle's demand, "that characters should be appropriate. A character may be manly, but it is not appropriate for a woman to be manly. . . ."[24] In seventeenth-century criticism this same demand for plausibility of types was governed by the theory of Decorum, which will be discussed shortly.

EXPRESSION

It will be realized that the difference between Hercules and Apollo, in the instance cited, would call for not only a distinction of physical type, but also for a marked difference of emotional expression. The struggling Hercules must reflect the passions of his battle, while Apollo might appear serene in his chariot. To determine the just expression of such figures the artist would be led again by his reason to consider the relation of his character types to the situation in which they were shown. A particular character, Achilles for instance, if shown in battle would reasonably be expected to display savage emotions; if he were painted with no indication of his passions, his "appropriate character" would not be fulfilled.

Emotions were to be shown by the pose of the figures, by gestures, and by facial expressions. The figures were considered as so many actors in the drama of the picture. Leonardo had stated this thesis, suggesting that painters imitate the expressive actions of the deaf,[25] and du Fresnoy was content to echo this idea: ". . . let the Figures to which Art cannot give a Voice, imitate the Mutes in their Actions."[26] These suggestions refer the artist directly to defective nature (the deaf and the mute), which was not consistent with the trend to acknowledge only nature's perfections. The leader of the French Academy, Charles Le Brun, offered a solution to this dilemma by illustrating the physical manifestations of various emotions as Descartes had described them in *Les Passions de l'Âme* (Amsterdam, 1649).[27] These illustrations codified emotional facial expressions; the physical types as drawn might be considered as definitive norms, as ideal types. In this way even the extremes of passion might be reconciled with the philosophy of the golden mean.

A little later than Le Brun's publication was the effort to determine ideal types of facial expression by reading them from Raphael's pictures, and in the eighteenth century this became customary. Mengs had maintained that Raphael would give the true "Taste of Expression," and shortly after the middle of the century the faces in Raphael's tapestry Cartoons were engraved and captioned with phrases descriptive of specific emotions.[28]

West probably knew Le Brun's illustrations of the passions, though he does not mention them. Certainly he was aware of the classicist's need to find ideal forms capable of expressing emotions, for he spoke of "the principles of philosophic study . . . reflection on the moral powers or passions of man," which would yield these.[29] But it was not the philosopher Descartes, or the painter-philosopher Le Brun, whom he credited with the discovery of perfected emotional expression. For him the great painter and great philosopher was Leonardo da Vinci: "As a painter, he not only went far beyond his predecessors, but laid down those principles of science in the expression of individual character, and of a soul and figure specifically and completely appropriated to each other . . . and by his knowledge of these principles, his expression of character became perfected."[30] For West, ideal character and emotional expression could be evolved from particular nature towards a nature at once universal and passionately expressive. He also found this same harmony between specific emotional expression and universal nature in Raphael's Cartoons. They were exemplary in showing "the various modes of reasoning, speaking, and feeling; but so blended with nature and truth, and so precise and determined in character, that criticism has nothing wherewith in that respect to ask for amendment."[31] The "philosophical" judgment which West advanced as supplying the criteria to transmute passions into their ideal forms of expression rested in practice upon the theory of Decorum.

DECORUM

The idea of Decorum, or fitness, was of considerable aid in determining the appearances of ideal nature, character, and expression. Decorum functioned on two planes, recommending first whatever was plausible to reason, and second whatever was appropriate to moral and social convention. In its first capacity it defended "natural," or probable appearances. A picture illustrating any text should account for appropriate racial types and customs, while costumes and setting also should be correct for the time and place indicated in the story.[32] But even more fundamentally the artist was instructed, "In all things you are to follow the order of Nature; for which Reason you must beware of drawing or painting Clouds, Winds and Thunder towards the Bottom of your Piece . . . but let every thing be set in its proper Place."[33]

West's most notable use of the theory of Decorum was the argument he presented to Reynolds for painting modern costumes on the figures in his "Death of General Wolfe" (Pl. 5). Reynolds urged the use of classical draperies, but West said, "I began by remarking that the event intended to be commemorated took place on the 13th of September, 1758, in a region of the world unknown to the Greeks and Romans, and at a period of time when no such nations, nor heroes in their costume, any longer existed. . . . but if, instead of the facts of the transaction, I represent classical fictions, how shall I be understood by posterity!"[34]

In its second capacity, Decorum dictated whatever was morally and socially acceptable, exercising censorship upon the artists' conceptions. The requirements of classic tragedy, "which employs the whole Forces of her Art in the main Action," were cited to show how the "trivial, foreign, or improper" must be rejected.[35] The artist should avoid also all things "obscene, impudent, filthy, unseemly, cruel, fantastical, poor and wretched,"[36] because in their avoidance he served the ethical aim of art and preserved physical beauty.

Decorum touched upon the determination of ideal character and emotional expression by advocating fitness to social conventions. In ancient times ideal nature had been drawn from men of heroic achievement but, due to courtly patronage of the arts in the Renaissance and Baroque eras, kings and courtiers had usurped the place of the hero. Somewhat snobbishly, de Piles could write, "The *Joy* of a *King* ought not to resemble that of a *Serving-man*: And the *Fierceness* of a *private Soldier* must not be like that of an *Officer*."[37] In this way Decorum might easily become a fallible guide by tending to dictate according to contemporary prejudice and current fashion. This was especially true when fine distinctions were drawn between social classes as in the eighteenth century. Indeed, Decorum could be deceptive in pointing up what seemed "natural" in daily life and so leading away from ideal nature. However, this danger was not great because Decorum, the sense of what is fitting and just, was itself subject to Taste, the ruling principle of art, and this Taste was formed upon antique culture. Ideally Decorum served simply to re-enforce the standards established by the love of classic art.

Finally, it must be noted that the classicist's theory did not maintain that genius could be supplied by rules. This contention is a modern misconception, for though there were rules for acquiring taste, and practical rules for how to paint, genius was acknowledged to be a gift from heaven. Precepts were given the artist, not to "stifle the Genius by a jumbled Heap of Rules," but because "Science perfects Genius;

and also moderates that Fury of the Fancy which cannot contain it self within the Bounds of Reason."[38] Such was exactly West's opinion when he first addressed the Royal Academy. He said the aim of the Academy was to supply "right instruction," but that the student should remain "perfectly free to that line and that expression of art which the natural turn of his own genius shall lead him to embrace."[39]

Although the theory of art, summarized above, has been long outmoded, there is much to recommend it. It was logical and convincing in structure, and it granted art an end as significant as the aims of philosophy and ethics. Art could elevate and improve mankind by revealing perfect goodness, truth, and beauty. Nor was it as confining in its limitations as is often believed today. A liberal practitioner, working within its tenets, could find scope for a wide variety of expression. Proof of this is offered by the varied modes of expression which West himself demonstrated in the course of his development. His theory shows him to have remained a classicist throughout his life, but his art responded sensitively to the demands of his age and to his personal interests. The latitude which he found within the limits of the theory will be seen in the several phases of his mature development.

WEST AND EUROPEAN TRADITION

Soon after West settled in England he developed a style completely in sympathy with the classicizing taste already described as a blend of traditional art theory with the new enthusiasm for ancient sculpture. His aims barely differed from the idealistic esthetics of the previous century; theoretically there was no difference, but in practice he tried to imitate ancient sculpture more objectively than had his predecessors.

The resulting mixture of sculptural imitation and traditional idealism is evident in his "Choice of Hercules" (Pl. 20). Here the central figure is strongly reminiscent of the "Vatican Meleager" (Pl. 21) in both pose and physique. Although the pose has been reversed, its essentials are preserved and, significantly, the outstretched hand in the picture is lost in shadow while the comparable hand is missing from the statue. One might expect that West would have modeled his Hercules after the "Farnese Hercules," which was considered the most perfect embodiment of the ancient demigod, but he would have been justified in departing from it because it shows an elderly Hercules and he was illustrating an episode from the hero's youth. Even so, West must have had a pang of conscience, for he arranged the legs of his figure after the fashion of the Farnese model.

With the stimulus of the ancient sculpture West combined the instruction of the learned art treatises. In this case his picture was motivated by the Earl of Shaftesbury's essay on taste, *The Judgment of Hercules* (London, 1714). He follows Shaftesbury's advice in illustrating exactly the moment in Prodicus' story of Hercules' choice between Virtue and Pleasure,[40] when the dispute for his favor is "already far advanc'd and Virtue seems to gain her cause." Hercules turns towards Virtue in West's Picture, while Pleasure's weak gesture reveals her as the loser of the contest. Shaftesbury recommended a "supine Air and Character of Ease and Indolence" for Pleasure, but Virtue must stand erect with one leg "rais'd on a broken piece of ground or rock," and her hands should show her feelings clearly, one hand "turn'd either upwards to the rocky Way mark'd out by her with approbation, or to the Sky or Stars in the same sublime sense, or downward . . . against *Pleasure* her-self."

41

West incorporated Shaftesbury's ideas into his picture without duplicating a picture by Matteis on the same subject painted under the influence of Shaftesbury.[41] The description of Virtue (gesturing both to the heavens and downward to depreciate her rival, while one of her feet is raised on an eminence of the ground) is so close to West's illustration that one must assume he had read the essay attentively with the idea of illustrating it. He modernized Matteis' version by his more careful imitation of ancient sculpture, and so introduced the new reverence for antique marbles which he had absorbed in Rome under the influence of Mengs and Winckelmann. The statuesque quality of his Hercules is of the type praised by Winckelmann for poised, calm "sedate grandeur." West's aim, then, is clear; he will carry on the traditional classicist's idealism as represented in Shaftesbury's morally pointed essay, but he will attempt to revitalize the tradition by a strict return to the classic style in the types and attitudes of his figures. This is the aim of his Stately Mode, and, as an esthetic intention, it determined his choice of themes, his figure style, and his compositional arrangements. These aspects of his first mature manner of painting will be examined now in turn.

THEMES

The sources of West's subject matter were varied, for he liberally interpreted the seventeenth-century theorists' admonition to search history for its notable episodes. He drew themes from ancient, medieval, and modern times, and he illustrated mythology, literature, biblical lore, and drama. Yet, as a classicist, West was drawn chiefly to two aspects of these stories, the heroic and the marvelous. In his pictures painted in the Stately Mode the theme of the hero predominated, because the hero, or heroine, most clearly exemplified all the requirements of academic idealism. The hero could incorporate the ideal of physical beauty with that of appropriate character in a superior physical type, and he might be relied upon to supply the necessary moral elevation. So a hero's noble deeds, for instance his clemency towards conquered subjects, formed an ideal theme. West painted such a subject for George III early in his career, "Cyrus Liberating the Family of Astyages" (Pl. 22). It illustrates how Cyrus, ruler of the Persians, received his father, Astyages, who had attempted to murder him as a child and, as king of the Medes, had opposed him in battle. Instead of wreaking vengeance, Cyrus takes him peaceably into his house.[42]

There probably were reasons in the current English political and economic situation for many of the heroic themes West painted. Patriotic heroism would certainly have been in Englishmen's minds after William Pitt became prime minister in 1756, for his determination to maintain England's supremacy in world trade demanded many sacrifices during the campaigns of conquest in North America, the West Indies, Africa, and India. An appropriate moral for the rising generation could be pointed up by a picture showing the theme of selfless, heroic dedication to a patriotic cause. West's first royal commission was for a picture with exactly this theme, "The Departure of Regulus" (Pl. 19).[43] It shows the Roman general Regulus, after his defeat in the first Carthaginian War, when he was escorted back to Rome. While there, he signified his willingness to return to Carthage and suffer certain death rather than have Rome sign a compromising treaty of surrender. Such a subject, which granted its actors the airs of noble

43

determination and melancholy, was admirably suited to the Stately Mode. It satisfied both present political needs and the demands of classical idealism.

A variant of the patriotic hero story is the theme of mourning for the lost national benefactor. "Agrippina Landing at Brundisium with the Ashes of Germanicus" (Pl. 1) and "Agrippina Mourning" (Pl. 25) are of this type, in which the calm, sorrowful attitudes of the figures fulfill the requirements of "sedate grandeur" with the added attraction of pathetic appeal.[44]

West also frequently painted the death of the hero. With the scene of Wolfe's death, "The Death of Epaminondas" (Pl. 27) and "The Death of the Chevalier Bayard" (Pl. 26) complete a trilogy of noble warriors' deaths, drawn from ancient, Renaissance, and modern history.[45] The latter two suggested themselves to West after his success with the picture of Wolfe, and George III eagerly commissioned them. The Epaminondas scene, showing the end of the Theban hero who overcame the Spartans at Mantinea in 362 B.C., has been treated with classic detail and restraint, but Bayard's death is illustrated with the strong emotionalism already noticed in "The Death of General Wolfe" (Pl. 5), an emotionalism which strained the limits of the Stately Mode.

Another related theme was the doomed warrior's farewell. "Hector Parting with his Wife and Child" (Pl. 28) emphasizes the union of pathos and antique grandeur so important for West's early success. Homer's most sympathetic figure in the *Iliad* is shown taking leave of his family before going out to meet the unvanquishable Achilles. [46] A similar moment is illustrated in "The Appeal to Coriolanus" (Pl. 23), for as Plutarch and Shakespeare tell, this remorseless hero lost his life soon after bidding farewell to his family. The appeal by his mother and wife prevented him from attacking Rome with the Volscians, who later killed him for his breach of faith.[47]

Besides paying tribute to the hero, West commemorated the heroine of myth and literature. He painted "Una and the Lion" (Pl. 30) to illustrate Spenser's *Faerie Queene* (I, iii, vi, 4), "O how can beautie maister the most strong." Classical goddesses, too, frequently inhabit his canvases, and are well represented in "Juno Receiving the Cestus from Venus" (Pl. 29), which shows an amusing episode from the *Iliad*. Juno borrows the girdle of love on a pretext of settling a family squabble between Ocean and Tethys, but she really intends to divert Jupiter's interest in the Trojan War.[48] Such goddesses offered unparalleled opportunities to paint idealized human beings, and West also capitalized on the traditional theme of the loves of the gods with the same end in view. "Venus Lamenting the Death of Adonis" (Pl. 31) combines a goddess with the fairest of mortals.[49]

The same search for ideal figures is also answered by West's allegorical personifications. He used several symbolic beings in the decorations done for the Royal Academy and now installed in the vestibule of Burlington House. A pleasant example is "Air" (Pl. 32), representing one of the four elements.

A theme which played a modest part in West's Stately Mode was the "Noble Savage." Unlike most of the others, this was not of traditional, but of current interest. Since the savage was considered noble, he became an ideal man, and might qualify as proper material for the classicizing artist. The notion that man had been healthier, happier, and nobler in early phases of his development was popularized in Rousseau's writings, and similar ideas were made current in England by Lord Monboddo.[50] Rousseau praised man's pastoral stage of culture, while Monboddo found his Utopia in the primitive age of ancient Greece. Monboddo especially emphasized the study of existing primitive societies, because he felt they might shed light upon the evolution of man.[51] West, it will be remembered, was familiar with the American Indians, and these "noble savages" appear sometimes in his pictures. Besides the well known examples in "The Death of General Wolfe" and "Penn's Treaty" (Plates 5 and 35), they are found in West's illustrations for William Smith's publication about the Ohio Indians.[52] In the example reproduced here (Pl. 34) it is amusing to notice the nobility and even classical affinity of the Indian who delivers an oration with all the force and dignity of a Roman senator, obviously stirring and impressing his European audience.

In a portrait of "Colonel Guy Johnson" (Pl. 33) West has included another Indian who might be Joseph Brant, the famous Mohawk chief. Brant fought with Johnson in the French and Indian Wars, and served as his secretary when Johnson was made superintendent of Indian Affairs in the colonies. But the figure of the Indian is hardly individualized enough to have been an actual portrait;[53] rather West seems to have intended this idealized Indian to symbolize the "noble savage." Details which bear out such an interpretation are the peace pipe, to which the Indian points, as opposed to the gun in the Englishman's hand, and the idyllic scene of Indian family life in the background. West was far less concerned with apt characterization of his subjects' faces than with the moral to be derived from the example of primitive man. His portrait has really become a "history piece," with the Indian hovering inspirationally behind the seated minister in a way analogous to the angels who inspire the Evangelists in medieval miniatures.

Themes like those listed above, illustrating the calmly dignified figures West favored during his early years in London, indicate not only particular subject interests but also stylistic intentions; subject and style are bound together in any work of art, they are codeterminants of the final effect of the work. These themes, stressing either pathetic moments in the life of a hero or his nobility of action and thought, are so persistent in West's early English paintings, that they must be considered essential to his first major style, the Stately Mode. To pursue this style further, his figure types and compositional arrangements must be examined next.

FIGURE STYLE

As noticed in the "Choice of Hercules" (Pl. 20) the figures in West's Stately Mode tend to follow the types and poses of ancient statues. "Pylades and Orestes" (Pl. 9) offers an excellent opportunity to study his method of adaptation. When the poses of West's two heroes in the picture are compared with those of the central figures in an Orestes sarcophagus (Pl. 10),[54] it becomes obvious that West used the ancient example as authority for his illustration; he has simply reversed the positions of the two figures, and their attitudes have been preserved with little modification. He has improved the physical appearance of his heroes, rounding their forms more subtly and proportioning them more pleasingly than the crude sarcophagus forms. The Hadrianic "Antinoos" figures come to mind as possible prototypes,[55] but the same style would have been known from many classical statues. Other parts of the sarcophagus relief were modified: the tree with its grim human remains was omitted, and the place of sacrifice was implied simply by the elegant little altar; the burning brazier and the statue of Diana were retained, but their style was improved. It may have struck West, then, that one of Raphael's Cartoons, "The Sacrifice at Lystra" (Pl. 11)[56] contained certain analogous aspects; it, too, showed a sacrificial procession which was being halted. It presents such close parallels with West's picture that there is little doubt he took hints from it. In both pictures the figures who wish to stop the procession appear upon a step at the left of the similarly placed altars; in both, the composition is terminated by sharply receding architecture at the left, and one's eye is led back to a pedestalled statue behind it. Add to these the patterned ground planes, and the crowds surging in from the right, and one may feel confident that West modeled his picture upon Raphael's Cartoon. With these strong reminders of the Antique and of Raphael, West was assured of the classical tradition.

When West did not use actual sculptural prototypes for his figures in the Stately Mode, he favored works in which the forms are modeled in a three-dimensional, sculpturesque way. His "Departure of Regulus" (Pl. 19) again recalls Raphael's figures, particularly those in the Cartoon, "Christ Giving the Keys to Peter," in the Victoria and Albert Museum. Also the strongly plastic modeling of the Carracci is often suggested by West's figures (see Plates 25, 29, and 31). This Bolognese manner is particularly evident in "St. Peter Denying Christ" (Pl. 36) as will be seen when it is compared with Ludovico Carracci's "Christ and the Woman of Canaan" (Pl. 37). Facial types, gestures, light and shadow, and mood are all remarkably similar.

To explain the satisfaction these figure types gave to people in West's day, to see how they seemed to transcend the reality of "common nature," the theory of ideal beauty should be recalled. To determine the form appropriate to any figure, the painter had to consider stature, build, coloration, temperament, and many other modifying factors in the figures he was to paint. Yet his heroes must be shown at their maximum perfection, raised above individual peculiarities to become universal types. The achievement of such conceptions, at once particular and universal, made an extraordinary demand upon the artist's imaginative capacity. Raphael enjoyed his enormous popularity because of his success in imaginatively intensifying every character he painted until each took on a grandeur of form which seemed to imply universality. This was the reason, too, that so many ancient statues, which are regarded today as insipid copies, were glorified in West's time. They possessed a secret life in the imaginations of this age; they embodied that magical intensification of common nature which raised it to an Olympian sphere. Their lack of expression and their repetitious attitudes were forgotten, for these ancient marbles appeared as supreme imaginative creations, bringing insight into eternal truth. To grasp the spell once cast by such frigid figures, it is helpful to cite Winckelmann's explanation: "For, the more tranquility reigns in a body, the fitter it is to draw the true character of the soul; which in every excessive gesture, seems to rush from her proper center, and being hurried away by extremes becomes unnatural, wound up to the highest pitch of passion, she may force herself upon the duller eye; but the true sphere of her action is simplicity and calmness."[57] This was the ideal incorporated by West in the figures of his Stately Mode. The use of them in his early pictures seems all the more deliberate in view of his later development, for in his second style he shows his interest in the very "highest pitch of passion."

COMPOSITION

The Stately Mode exhibits two distinct compositional systems, which may be named after their sources, the Raphaelesque and the Bolognese. The first type was reserved generally for various heroic themes, while the Bolognese manner served usually for religious and mythological subjects.

West's most frequent early method of composing was borrowed from the type made famous by Raphael in the frescoes of the Sala della Segnature. "The School of Athens" is characteristic of this type in which the picture has been conceived like a stage, with the main action shown upstage center, and the supporting actors grouped at either side, downstage. This way of arranging figures was followed by many artists after Raphael, notably by Domenichino and Poussin. There is, of course, a difference in the way the artists of the Renaissance and of the seventeenth century painted this stagelike space, for a far more convincing feeling of spatial recession is found in the later works,[58] but despite this very important distinction, the convention of the picture as a stage with actors ranged across it in planes parallel with the picture surface, has remained essentially the same. This general system also appeared in a great deal of Italian and French works, so the sources from which West might have drawn it are too various to allow specific identification. Perhaps the work of Raphael is indicated as his source by the fact that when West used this compositional arrangement, as in "Agrippina Landing" (Pl. 1), or in the picture of Regulus (Pl. 19) he did not achieve that clear spatial recession so characteristic of the seventeenth-century masters.

A modification of this Raphaelesque composition may be seen in

"Penn's Treaty with the Indians" (Pl. 35)[59] where receding buildings in the background give a slightly greater emphasis upon deep space. But these recessional forms are not emphasized, nor are the receding planes on the figures stressed. The picture tends to become a series of silhouette planes which are established by the grouping of figures and by the background forms. This system is best known in Poussin's painting, which clearly influenced West.

There is a curious paradox in West's early method of modeling his figures, for they are carefully, sculpturesquely modeled, but at the same time they are posed and shaded so as to minimize their recessional planes. This may be seen in "Penn's Treaty," where the groups at either side are given a maximum lateral extension to maintain them in a plane parallel with the surface of the canvas. Or again in the group of Indians, notice how often one's eye is confronted by a flat plane, so that one looks straight into a shoulder, or a chest, instead of passing beyond the figures into free space. Even the folds of drapery in the Quakers' costumes are disposed at the left like a curtain to cut off interest in the space extending behind them. Possibly West may have felt this kind of "frontality" (of modeling, more than of posing) was necessary to give a greater feeling of importance to his figure groups; attention is held on the groups instead of being allowed to escape beyond them (cf. Plates 1, 19, and 22).

Another modification of the Raphaelesque system will be seen in "Pylades and Orestes" (Pl. 9). The space is still conceived as stagelike, but the main figures have been moved downstage, and the center of action shifted to one side. The shallower depth in which the actors move processionally across the canvas suggests an origin in ancient relief sculpture. This is probably ultimately true, but, as mentioned above, West was imitating Raphael's Cartoon and his work is closer to this than to antique bas-reliefs.

It is inviting to speculate that perhaps West's return to Raphael-esque compositions was a deliberate reaction against the facility of seventeenth-century spatial composing, a reform campaign which he led against "Baroque" tendencies. But little positive evidence could be cited to support this theory. It seems more probable that the similarity between West's compositional methods and those of Raphael and his followers is simply the result of imitating Raphaelesque prototypes. The occasional resemblance to antique relief composition, as in the center group of "Agrippina Landing" (Pl. 1), is probably also due to imitation, rather than to any deliberate reaction against the painting of the previous century. This is confirmed as one continues the study of West's compositional methods, because the next type to be noticed shows West quite willing to carry on a Baroque rather than a Renaissance or ancient style.

Besides the Raphaelesque types of composition in his Stately Mode, West often used a scheme from the seventeenth-century Bolognese school, as may be seen in his "Hagar and Ishmael" (Pl. 38). Its Bolognese affinity is evident in the smoothly modeled faces and voluminous draperies, recalling the Carracci and their followers. Its composition carries on the formula of the miracle pictures so popular in that school; Lanfranco's well known "Ecstasy of St. Margaret" in the Pitti Gallery is particularly brought to mind.

The distinctive features of the Bolognese compositional scheme are the apparent nearness of the figures and the use of forms receding diagonally into the pictorial space. Since this is a Baroque rather than a Renaissance type of composing, the space is undefined as a stage or box; instead space receives its definition from the figures which apparently move through it, and so imply its extension. This undefined spatial setting is especially effective for the theme of Hagar and Ishmael, because it heightens the feeling of desolation in the wilderness to which Hagar and her son were sent.

As West matured he became more adept at implying space by diagonally receding forms. His "Ascension of Our Saviour" (Pl. 39), for instance, is quite successful in this respect. It follows Bolognese tradition closely, as a comparison with Ludovico Carracci's "Transfiguration" (Pl. 40) will prove. Both pictures share the fundamental Baroque conception of space, and both even show a general similarity in the distribution of figures. An upper and lower register, with figures of nearly equal size in each, is characteristically Bolognese, as are also the gesturing arms and upturned faces, which establish a psychological connection between the two registers. In the second phase of his style, which West's "Ascension of Our Saviour" anticipates in many ways, the Baroque rather than the Raphaelesque compositional method became dominant.

Some elements in West's early style bear similarities to the art of Titian and Correggio. The influence of these painters was probably absorbed at first hand when West visited Venice and Parma, but he combined it with those aspects of ancient sculpture and of Raphael's style which he admired, so that the mixture resembles the eclecticism of the Bolognese Academy or that of Mengs. For this reason Titian and Correggio cannot be cited as certainly determining his style. For example "Una and the Lion" (Pl. 30) recalls the Venetians, Giorgione and Titian, but it might also have been suggested by Bolognese works such as Domenichino's. One can only say that Venetian coloring and

Parmesan light and shade are common to both the Bolognese and West.

The Stately Mode ranged in coloring from brilliant hues, which impressed Horace Walpole as similar to Barocci's manner,[60] to dull colors with brown shades predominant. Bright colors are used vividly in "The Appeal to Coriolanus" (Pl. 23), but as West developed, these were soon muted to more somber, but still rich color harmonies. Venetian or Bolognese in origin, these colors may be seen in the two pictures of Agrippina (Plates 1 and 25) and in that of Regulus (Pl. 19). At other times, as in "Penn's Treaty" (Pl. 35), the color was somber, indicating a solemn mood. But there is not always a correspondence between mood and coloring, nor did West devote one type of coloring to classical themes, and another to battle pieces, etc. Thus "The Death of General Wolfe" is surprisingly bright in color, though here there is a certain deep resonance in the vivid hues which is reconcilable with the tragic theme. As one might expect, an appropriateness of coloring with theme seems to have been aimed at, but West did not follow rigid prescriptions in his choice of colors.

West's first mature style brought to London the latest cultured taste of Rome. It carried on the traditions of Humanist art and innovated a new restraint in the actions and expressions of the painted figures. Its qualities do ample credit to West's grasp of the leading trends in European culture. How he modified his style, again in sympathy with the most progressive critical thought of his time, will be seen now in turning to his second style.

CHAPTER THREE

THE DREAD MANNER

——————————— ✳ ———————————

ESTHETIC BACKGROUND

ABOUT twenty years after West began painting in England his style slowly underwent a radical change which can be accounted for by the influence of current English esthetic ideas. His contact with these ideas came from Edmund Burke's popular treatise on the Sublime and the Beautiful,[1] as will be shown later when the effect of Burke's Sublime on West's painting is studied. First, a brief definition of Burke's critical standards must be made in order to clarify the new aims of West's second style.

Following the lead of British Empiricists, Burke turned his interest from classical concepts of universal nature to direct perception of nature's particulars.[2] His concern was to analyze the perceptions and reflective notions produced by various objects and situations in daily experience. He rejected the classicist's theory that beauty was a quality of an object,[3] and claimed that beauty resided in the pleasurable emotions which objects or events might occasion. In this way the field of esthetics was redefined, and beauty was found in feelings instead of in objects. Yet the qualities of objects were still believed to be fundamental in giving rise to emotions, so that Burke defined beauty as the feeling caused by objects which were small, smooth, gradually varied in form, delicate, and softly colored.[4] Conversely, the Sublime was said to be produced by whatever was great, rough, irregular, powerful, and heavily shaded.[5] These objective properties were only significant because they could produce emotions by causing pleasant or painful feelings.

The feelings which every object or event excited functioned through three channels: sense perception, mental association, and intuitive sympathy. Through these everything, which was not a matter of indifference, was transported to the imagination, "the most extensive province of pleasure and pain."

The first of these channels, sense perception, was believed to produce pleasure or pain by the physiological structure and functions of the sense organs; certain sensations were pleasant because they relaxed the strain in eye or ear, but others were painful irritants, which overworked the senses and caused pain.[6] These physical pleasures or pains were considered productive of mental states, frames of mind, or feelings, which determined emotional response. This belief, that direct perceptions ultimately caused emotions, followed necessarily from the Empiricist premise that the mind was a *tabula rasa* devoid of all ideas and emotional reactions until these were implanted by perception and retained by memory.

The second channel by which external nature operated upon the mind was association of the immediately observed object with remembered ideas and sensations. A psychology called associationism, originating in Aristotle, was revived to show how the mind functioned according to certain patterns of association.[7] While all knowledge was admitted to be the result of perception, the mind had a reflective capacity to arrange and combine the sensuous images it received. This arrangement was not subject to whim, but was directed by certain patterns of normal mental behaviour. When viewing an object one would associate similar objects formerly experienced, or, conversely, by a principle of opposition, objects remembered whose characteristics were directly opposite to those of the object perceived. One might associate ideas suggested by the principles of cause and effect, or one might be reminded of other objects or events contiguous in time and space with previous similar experiences. Through these modes of association any given experience might prove pleasing or painful according to the pattern of remembered pleasure or pain. So associationism gave another key to emotional response, and provided an arational, instinctive basis for understanding the relationship between object and feeling. Burke showed his willingness to accept both perception and association as sources of emotional reactions when he wrote, "But as it must be allowed that many things affect us after a certain manner, not by any natural powers they have for that purpose, but by association; so it would be absurd, on the other hand, to say that all things affect us by association only; since some things must have been originally and naturally agreeable or disagreeable, from which the others derive their associated powers. . . ."[8]

The third channel linking the objective world with inner emotional response was sympathy. This will be more fully discussed in the next chapter as background for West's last style of painting, but here it should be described briefly as forming part of Burke's theory.

In the eighteenth century the word sympathy was often used, as it is today, to mean compassion, but the term basically meant empathy—a spontaneous assimilation of the emotions observed in others. By sympathy one could experience all the emotions of a character in life, in a drama, novel, or picture. This vicarious experience was believed to be as vivid and actual as the original emotion. As Burke said, "It is by this principle chiefly that poetry, painting, and the other affecting arts, transfuse their passions from one breast to another. . . ."[9]

The pleasurable and painful experiences gathered by perception, association, and sympathy were the sources of beauty and sublimity. Burke connected beauty with pleasure and the Sublime with threatening experiences of pain, but in the latter case he was led into the difficult position of claiming fear to be the source of an enjoyable emotion, sublimity. To solve this paradox he marshaled two arguments showing "how pain can be a cause of delight."[10] First, he argued, the act of exercising perception, association, and sympathy was in itself satisfying: "Providence has so ordered it, that a state of rest and inaction, however it may flatter our indolence, . . . should generate such disorders, as may force us to have recourse to some labor, as a thing absolutely requisite to make us pass our lives with tolerable satisfaction. . . . Labor . . . is equally necessary to these finer and more delicate organs, on which, and by which, the imagination and perhaps the other mental powers act."[11] Secondly, he recalled an interpretation of katharsis to explain how terror, or fear of pain, might be delightful: ". . . if the pain and terror are so modified as not to be actually noxious . . . as these emotions clear the parts, whether fine or gross, of a dangerous and troublesome incumberance, they are capable of producing delight; not pleasure, but a sort of delightful horror, a sort of tranquillity tinged with terror. . . ."[12] By exercising the emotions, "delightful horror" could purge the mind of actually painful sensations and associations. This idea made possible Burke's fundamental thesis that the Sublime was rooted in the powerful emotion of terror.

Burke found the origins of beauty and sublimity in instinctive rather than in rational reactions. Pleasure, which was the source of beauty, he grounded in man's sexual and social instincts; terror, the source of the Sublime, played upon man's instinct for self-preservation. Instinctive reactions were seen as the mainspring of esthetic response, but like all English eighteenth-century writers on taste, Burke could not entirely forgo the role of rational judgment in forming his critical standards. Judgment was necessary, he thought, to choose what associative patterns were esthetically best: "But as many of the works of imagination are not confined to the representation of sensible objects, nor to efforts upon the passions, but extend themselves to the manners, the characters, the actions, and designs of men, their relations, their virtues and vices, they come within the province of the judgment, which is improved by attention, and by the habit of reasoning. All these make a very considerable part of what are considered the objects of taste; and Horace sends us to the schools of philosophy and the world for our instruction in them."[13] Burke maintained a strong heritage from classicizing criticism in his reliance upon rational judgment to reveal moral good in various aspects of life and art. In fact, he did not reject all classicizing standards; rather he explored certain aspects of taste which had been glossed over in seventeenth-century critical writing. By placing his emphasis upon intuitional instead of rational sources of esthetic pleasure he was able to make a significant contribution, extending the esthetic field to include the "terrible sublime." There were many other writers in England who were interested in the

Sublime, many who had been stimulated by translations of the ancient treatise on rhetoric, *Longinus On the Sublime*,[14] and the trend towards less rigidly rational principles of taste was widespread. But, although Burke was criticized for too narrow a definition of sublimity,[15] it was his treatise, despite its fallacies, which made the Sublime an essential part of esthetic criticism, and, moreover, made the Sublime a popular concept. The various qualities of Burke's Sublime will be more fully described now as their relation to West's second style of painting is indicated.

RELATION TO BURKE'S SUBLIME

The transposition of Burke's ideas on the Sublime into an esthetic for the painter would not have been difficult, for as Burke said, "the images in painting are exactly similar to those in nature. . . ."[16] Since he had defined the causes of sublimity from external nature, he had also effectively determined them for the imitative arts.

Burke himself had no great fondness for painting, much preferring poetry, which he believed could stir the imagination far more profoundly. Poetry offered a highly desirable obscurity and confusion of imagery which seemed to him more stimulating to grand ideas than clearly defined images in painting. He described his preference in this way: "To represent an angel in a picture, you can only draw a beautiful young man winged: but what painting can furnish out anything so grand as the addition of one word, 'the angel of the *Lord*'? It is true, I have here no clear idea; but these words affect the mind more than the sensible image did. . . ."[17] One wonders if West could have taken these words as a challenge to the painter, and produced his spirited "Archangel Gabriel" (Pl. 41) to refute Burke's charge. The picture was exhibited at the Royal Academy with the title, paraphrasing a verse in Revelation, chapter 10, "A mighty angel standeth upon the land and upon the sea."[18] As an image it is eminently sublime in all the terms Burke established. The following digest of Burke's requirements for sublimity may profitably be compared with West's picture:

Emotions stirred by the Sublime: astonishment, admiration, reverence, awe.

Sources of the Sublime: terror, obscurity, power, privation (vacuity, darkness, solitude, silence), vastness, infinity, repetition (giving an artificial sense of infinity), difficulty, magnificence, Deity.

Physical characteristics of the Sublime: great size, rugged, irregular forms, darkness, strong contrasts of light and dark, spaciousness, suddenness.

It is remarkable that out of this extensive list only "difficulty" is entirely excluded from application to the picture. Otherwise the painting seems almost an illustration of Burke's thesis. This strong affinity between West's picture and Burke's Sublime suggests that West actually used the essay on the Sublime and Beautiful as a painter's handbook, extracting from it indications of the kind of emotions that a picture should arouse, and specific directions for arousing them. This suspicion becomes a conviction when his "Death on the Pale Horse" (Pl. 45) is compared with Burke's specifications, for a striking series of analogies are presented.

One of the best links between Burke's theory and "Death on the Pale Horse" is found in West's conception of his central figure, Death, which is veiled in obscurity, wears a crown on his head, and flashes bolts of lightning from his hand. Compare this image with Milton's description of Death, a description which Burke quoted:

> The other shape,
> If shape it might be call'd that shape had none
> Distinguishable, in member, joint, or limb;
> Or substance might be call'd that shadow seem'd;
> For each seem'd either; black he stood as night;
> Fierce as ten furies; terrible as hell;
> And shook a deadly dart. What seem'd his head
> The likeness of a kingly crown had on.

Burke maintained, "In this description all is dark, uncertain, confused, terrible, and sublime to the last degree."[19] Admittedly, West might have read this in Milton's poem, instead of in Burke's treatise, but West never painted any other Miltonic subject.[20] Perhaps he was warned of Milton's heterodoxy by his friends among the clergy, but, at any rate, it would be curious to find him singling out this one passage, unless it was suggested to him by Burke.

The picture affords many other parallels with Burke's Sublime. Its darkness of coloring, and its confusion of struggling forms, reflect Burke's contention that obscurity and confused images were main sources of sublimity. Eternity was implied in the theme of the apocalyptic Horsemen, and infinity conveyed by the measureless depths of the background, filling "the mind with that delightful horror which is the . . . truest test of the sublime."[21] Vastness, too, was accounted for in the very size of the canvas (177" x 551"). Burke's fundamental thesis, that sublimity springs from the instinct of self-preservation, was indeed the whole theme of the picture: a "family of rank" in the center foreground struggles unavailingly against the crushing hoofs of Death's pale charger, men and beasts contend in mortal combat, a man is tossed aloft on the horns of a bull,[22] while in the sky other episodes of destruction are in progress, recalling the omens of evil frequently mentioned by Homer and Virgil. In the left background a lover is struck dead by lightning, and at the right Roman soldiers are despoiling the temple at Jerusalem, symbolizing the destructions of war. Burke's requirement of irrational power is amply echoed in West's painting of savage animals. Burke made specific reference to horses; provided their usefulness was forgotten, they might qualify as sublime, "whose neck is clothed with thunder, the glory of whose nostrils is terrible, who swalloweth the ground with fierceness and rage."[23] Such a memorably irrational description fits West's Pale Horse remarkably, for it is shown emerging from thunderous clouds in a mad, helter-skelter activity. Its implied violent movement indicates the ferocity of uncontrolled power, well calculated to inspire terror.

Burke also discussed the sublimity of Deity, which is paralleled in West's picture by the figure of the godhead as the first of the Horsemen, riding off to the right-hand side. Burke's Privation as a source of sublimity might be answered by West's fleshless figure, rooting in the ground, to the left of Deity. While this is not an illustration of the privations Burke discussed, it is an obvious pictorial symbol for privation, and West may have intended it to convey this idea.

So detailed is the parallel between West's picture and Burke's theory that one may assume a deliberate effort by West to incorporate as much of Burke's "terrible sublime" as possible in this one picture. Nor was the correspondence lost upon the early spectators of West's huge canvas. When it was exhibited, about 1830, in America, a pamphlet was circulated with it, telling, "The general effect proposed to be excited by this Picture is the terrible sublime and its various modifications, until lost in the opposite extremes of pity and horror; a sentiment which painting has so seldom attempted to awaken, that a particular description of the subject will probably be acceptable to the Public.''[24] While the ensuing description in the pamphlet does not mention Burke as West's inspiration, it will be remembered that Burke was the promoter and popularizer of terror as the source of sublimity.

Because "Death on the Pale Horse" was a veritable *summa* of horrors, it reflected the new esthetic tastes of the eighteenth century as they were fused in Burke's theory. It depended for its effectiveness upon those psychologies based in perception, association, and sympathy which were outlined above. This is true even more of the earlier versions of the picture (Plates 42, 43, and 44), because they were more spontaneously designed, and the implication of movement is more convincing. Since the feeling of dread to be aroused in the spectator depended upon the relentlessness of motion in the plunging, frenzied horses and wild beasts, the more premeditated treatment of the forms in the late version is far less emotionally stimulating. Besides the lack of motion, several altered details in the picture of 1817 show an attempt on West's part to appeal more to reason than to emotion. Thus, the first of the Horsemen, who remained a fierce destructive bowman in the earlier pictures, has been recast in the last one as the Saviour, whose movement is majestic instead of headstrong. Also in the late version the head of the Pale Horse suggests the horse's head from the Parthenon pediment, which West knew among the Elgin marbles.[25] By the time this last version was painted, West had lost interest in Burke's terrible sublime, and had moved on to other preoccupations which determined his third, or Pathetic, style. Of the four versions, perhaps the drawing of 1783 is the most effective. Although it sacrifices "obscurity" by not having the darkly shaded areas of the paintings, and so loses one important element of Burke's Sublime, nevertheless the central family group is more emotively conceived. In the later pictures the mother is shown as already dead, and the original strong, protective gesture of the father has become one of despair. The youth who crouches behind the mother, and gestures despairingly as he cries to her, has been entirely disassociated from the family group in the later painted versions, and, as mentioned, seems to typify starvation in the final picture. Clearly, in the drawing the group is unified by a common emotional experience of terror, whereas the paintings have sacrificed much of the intensity originally calculated to play upon the observer's sympathy.

These earlier versions of "Death on the Pale Horse" show that West's interest in the terrible sublime considerably predated the picture of 1817. The drawing was done in 1783, and probably the first painted version was done soon afterwards.[26] The second painted picture cannot be considered a sketch, because West took it to France with him in 1802 to represent his style of painting.[27] This must have required considerable boldness, because when he went over to see Napoleon's art treasures and exhibited this work, he must have known that David's very different Neoclassical style was the approved mode in France. He may have wanted to show how he had already moved beyond the restraints of David's style.

Looking back upon West's development, it will be seen that 1783, the date of the drawing for "Death on the Pale Horse," seems to mark the opening of his chief interest in the terrible sublime. In fact, there are many pictures from this time onward which indicate his fascination with Burke's ideas, and some of these will be examined now to show how they were painted with the intention of arousing "delightful horror" in the spectator.

WEST'S INTERPRETATION OF THE SUBLIME

West's style of painting acquired new characteristics in response to Burke's Sublime, new qualities which distinguished a phase quite different from his earlier Stately Mode. Since this second phase reflected the notion that esthetic feelings arose from emotions of fear, terror, and awe, it may be termed the Dread Manner. A few of West's paintings, dating in the first half of the 1780's, led to the formation of this new style, while after about 1805 he seldom used it. During this period of over twenty years West did not abandon his earlier style entirely, for it was appropriate to stimulate gentle emotional reactions, but he was fascinated chiefly by subjects calculated to stir astonishment and reverent wonder, or to excite vicarious terror in the observer.

How West intended to arouse these lively passions may be demonstrated in "The Conversion of St. Paul" (Pl. 49) painted in 1786. Before it the spectator's eyes are impelled this way and that by the varied angles of torsos, arms, legs, and tilted heads. One's glance will emerge at last from the confusion of complex, interwoven forms below to rise towards the serenity of Christ's figure above. Such a striking contrast heightens the effectiveness of both parts of the illustration, but the major emphasis has been placed on the lower section with its astonished, terror-stricken witnesses to the miraculous apparition overhead. These figures demand first attention, and have been made prominent, because they are the agents by which the spectator's emotions will be moved, or exercised and purged of harmful content, as Burke had recommended. West's method of eliciting "terror" in the observer was not simply to frighten him by fearful images of omnipotent deity or of terrifying demons. Instead, he depended upon the theories of sympathy and association. West's picture invites the spectator to sympathize with the painted figures, to merge his emotions with those of the actors, who vividly display their feelings in pose, gesture, and facial expression. The observer is also expected to associate freely from his own previous experience of fear or wonder, and to evaluate the picture by the forcefulness with which it elicits sympathy and promotes a lively chain of associations to play through the mind. Sympathy and association of ideas were the premises of West's Dread Manner, as they were also of Burke's theories. Briefly stated, the theory of the Dread Manner was this: A figure, apparently under emotional stress as reflected in his action and expression, will awaken an identical emotion in the observer, subject to that observer's capacity to sympathize and associate ideas readily. Since terror was believed to be the strongest of all emotions, it would move most profoundly, enlisting the maximum sympathetic participation and the most vivid associations. West found several effective ways to sustain these reactions in his spectators. With his choice of intensely dramatic themes went a new way of visualizing details and composition, and even a distinctive way of handling his paint.

THEMES

In the second phase of his development West showed a preference for subjects taken from the Scriptures, especially from Revelation. The Bible became a more important source for illustration than the classical histories and myths, which had predominated in his earlier pictures, though "dread" themes might be found in both.[28] West's fondness for biblical subjects was furthered by his youthful experiences in Quaker society, which would have made him very familiar with Bible stories. His incentive to paint them was increased by a royal commission in 1780. George III and West agreed upon an extensive list of thirty-five subjects showing *Revealed Religion*, including stories from the Old and New Testaments. These pictures were to decorate New Chapel, Windsor Castle, and were nearly all finished or sketched by 1805.[29]

West's biblical pictures were not motivated primarily by religious feeling, but reflect his interest in grand subjects conformable to his ideas of the "terrible sublime." The appeal of the marvelous will be seen particularly in "Saul and the Witch of Endor" (Pl. 6) where the subject seems to have been chosen simply because of its macabre quality and its ability to arouse astonishment. It was painted in 1777, and so is a remarkably early example of that emotionalism which fascinated Barry, Fuseli, and Blake, and which became predominant in West's Dread Manner.[30]

The interests these pictures reveal extend beyond the reserve of West's Stately Mode, and prefigure concerns which occupied many later Romantic artists. Yet West's paintings in the Dread Manner will not be understood by the study of Romanticism. It must be remembered that in theory West remained faithful to the tenets of classicizing idealism; his admiration for antique art never abated, and he continued to imitate ancient works. Further, he never lost sight of the classicists' intention of idealizing his figures, nor of the basic assumption that art should be morally elevating. His Dread Manner is best understood when it is considered an extension of classicism to embrace new, more emotionally stirring themes and qualities. Certainly West would not have considered himself a "Romantic," since the term was not current in its present cultural sense. But had it been in use,

68

there is still too much latent classicism in West's thought and work for him to have accepted it.

Certain themes, as West painted them, mark a transition from the Stately Mode to the Dread Manner. Some of them promoted a more liberal interpretation of emotions than was acceptable for the Stately Mode, while others introduced broader interests with episodes from medieval and modern history. These led West to paint figure types, costumes, and other details which lay beyond the scope of strictly classicizing art. A royal commission for eight pictures on the history of Edward III,[31] to decorate the state rooms in Windsor Castle, forced upon West an idiom of medieval forms, and the effect of these pictures is distinct from the qualities of the Stately Mode. The preliminary oil sketch for one of these pictures, "Queen Philippa Interceding for the Burgesses of Calais" (Pl. 50), shows how West, although scarcely accurate in painting fourteenth-century costumes, has abandoned traditional classicizing drapery and detail, and has attempted to create the atmosphere of the Middle Ages. His figures have taken on a feeling of life and emotion which is foreign to his earlier style. The picture is not yet in the Dread Manner—the theme did not call for this—but it marks a transition towards the strong emotionalism and free handling of that style.

Others in the Windsor series, the battle scene of Crécy and "King Edward III Entertaining His Prisoners" (Plates 52 and 51) also capture a romantic flavor from the age of chivalry, and exhibit heightened emotionalism. While some details of these still recall Renaissance traditions, especially the horses in the battle pieces, nevertheless, they do not patently bring prototypes before one's eye as did so many of the earlier works. While they are not West's best productions, they show an

69

imaginative power on his part in illustrating stirring national events from the Middle Ages. They even anticipate battle scenes by Delacroix with their air of romance and medieval pageantry.

Another theme which appeared with increasing frequency in West's mature works was landscape. Although his interest in nature was not a part of his Dread Manner, it must be discussed here, since like the concern with "dread" themes, it developed with the changing critical standards outlined above in relation to Burke's Sublime. In short, landscape became a source of pleasurable feelings, being spoken of as sublime or beautiful, and so entered the esthetic field, which Burke and many other writers on taste were redefining. For West, landscape was never a serious rival of the history piece, or figure composition, but the eighteenth-century attitude towards nature, especially the theory of the picturesque, was important in determining his favorite treatment of backgrounds in the Dread Manner.

Several causes conspired together in England to create a widespread fascination with natural scenery. The Grand Tour introduced many Englishmen to the Arcadian views of Claude Lorrain, and to the rugged grandeur of nature in Salvator Rosa's pictures. These had great influence upon poets and painters, and produced that British zeal for landscape gardening so characteristic of cultured life in this time.[32] Concurrent with the growing fondness for an Italianate vision of nature, Flemish and Dutch landscape pictures were winning considerable popularity. As a glance at the contents of Walpole's *Anecdotes of Painting* confirms, many artists from Flanders and Holland found employment in England, and their works were eagerly collected.[33] While these northern painters often maintained an atmosphere of Virgilian Arcady, blending rustic figures with landscape, they stressed nature's irregularities and variety. Their trees were more angular, their paths more winding than those of Claude. Their effects were distinct, too, from the "sublimities" of Rosa's scenes, presenting views nearer to the Englishman's experience of his own countryside.

This interest in landscape painting became identified with the word picturesque: "a term expressive of that peculiar kind of beauty which is agreeable in a picture," as William Gilpin defined it.[34] Gilpin was the leading exponent of picturesque beauty, which became an important esthetic category, and considerably broadened critical judgment in West's period. In 1786 Gilpin published notes he had made when traveling in the mountain and lake district; he interspersed his comments on the countryside and its landmarks with ideas which formulated his theories on scenic beauty into a system. An ideally picturesque view should contain distant mountains, lakes in the middle distance, and a foreground of rocks, woods, broken grounds, valleys, cascades, or rivers. A lake's surface was admirably picturesque because it responded to a breeze, and like a "shattered mirror" seemed "tremblingly alive." Rocks were best when they exhibited "a fractured surface; which in general has a better effect than a smooth one." Gilpin emphasized variety and irregularity as the sources of picturesque beauty, but every part of a scene was not to be irregular in its forms, for this would defeat the need for variety. "In a *distance* the ruling character is *tenderness*; which on a *fore-ground*, gives way to what the painter calls *force*, and *richness*." So a broad treatment in soft, unbroken colors was appropriate in the background of a picture, while elsewhere the painter might use "those bold, those strong characteristic touches, which excite the imagination; and lead it to form half the picture, itself."[35]

An important aspect of Gilpin's picturesque beauty was its association with man's emotions. In speaking of the lake country, he said, "No tame country, however beautiful, however adorned, can distend the mind, like this aweful, and majestic scenery . . . as when rough with all its bold irregularities about it; when beauty, and deformity, grandeur and horror, mingled together, strike the mind with a thousand opposing ideas. . . ."[36] Gilpin's guide in his search for emotional associations drawn from natural scenery was Burke's *Sublime and Beautiful*, which he freely quoted in his own writings.[37] Burke's theories were also carried on by the country squire, Uvedale Price, who wrote of picturesque beauty under the more impressive term, "The Picturesque," and suggested that it was an esthetic category based on aspects of scenery and on associated mental states of feeling. It rested between Burke's two categories of beauty and sublimity.[38] Both Gilpin and Price treated their subjective preferences and feelings about landscape as if they were objective data, and tried to deduce from them an objective norm of picturesqueness.

The views of these authors, which constitute the popular theory of picturesque beauty, were contested in 1805 by Richard Payne Knight, who argued that Price should have distinguished between simple perceptions and emotional reactions which were the product of mental associations and feelings of sympathy.[39] Knight believed that Price had defined only visual pleasure in varied perceptions, but had fallen into error every time he associated perception with intellectual and emotional sentiments. But of these views, Gilpin's was the least encumbered with theoretical disputation, and probably remained the most popular.

West was Gilpin's cousin,[40] and would have had good opportunity to become familiar with Gilpin's ideas. Certainly he had Gilpin's fundamental criteria of variety in mind when he described the countryside about Bath to Joseph Farington: "He spoke of Bath & its vicinity with rapture as abounding with the picturesque Scenery.—Take Bath & 20 miles round it He sd. & there is not in the world anything superior to it. Rocks of the finest forms for the painter that He had ever seen,—large, square forms.—*Quarry's* worked out, now most picturesque & romantic. . . . Take *Tivoli away* & Rome & its vicinity of 20 miles not to be compared with Bath & its neighborhood."[41]

One of West's most pleasant pictures is the sketch, "View from the Terrace at Windsor" (Pl. 55), which preserves the fresh feeling of nature genuinely experienced. It gives a broad impression of the scene, generalized in the bold touches Gilpin would have admired. Its banks of clouds with their varied forms, and its modulated colors in the foliage also seem to echo Gilpin's suggestions. In another picture, "Woodcutters in Windsor Great Park" (Pl. 54), the requirements of broken grounds and irregular forms in the foreground, contrasted with the "breadth and repose" of the distance, are well illustrated.

The theory of the Picturesque did not move West to produce very many landscapes, but it probably called his attention to the emotive possibilities of landscape settings for his figure compositions. In his mature works he generally depended upon rugged rocks, the rapid alternation of light and shadow in irregularly formed cloud banks, and the vast expanses of distance to sustain the "dread" mood of his themes.

It will not be necessary to list here in detail the themes West particularly favored in the Dread Manner, since they will become evident in the course of the stylistic analysis. It will be enough to notice that they all dealt with miraculous events, supernatural forces, or super-human powers, and that they amply afforded him the opportunities to illustrate man's reactions to objects terribly sublime.

TREATMENT OF FIGURES

A general characteristic of most pictures in the Dread Manner was a new effect of strong movement in the forms. This intimation that the figures were in motion, often violently moving, was probably a response to "the great power of the sublime . . . [which] hurries us on by an irresistible force," as Burke expressed it.[42] While Burke was speaking figuratively, nevertheless he described an effect best supplied in painting by the implication of relentless motion. Consequently West's "Death on the Pale Horse" (Plates 42–45) was filled with lunging figures and animals, the central horse shown completely on the rampage. A similar expression of strenuous movement is found in most of the pictures West painted in the Dread Manner.

To achieve these agitated figures, West altered his pictorial sources from the calm classical statues and Raphaelesque motifs of his first style. Now he drew upon the more dramatic late classical art and extensively upon Rubens. Several general similarities exist between "Death on the Pale Horse" and Rubens' "Lion Hunt" (Pl. 46): both contain a wildly plunging "pale horse" in the center, trampled victims, men with upraised swords contending with lions, and a central rider with upward swirling drapery. West's imagination could easily have been stirred by the "Lion Hunt," because he had a print of it hanging in his drawing room.[43]

Another probable source for the composition of "Death on the

Pale Horse" is the drawing of an ancient sarcophagus (Pl. 47), in the collection at Windsor Castle, where West was a frequent visitor. The most striking analogy presented by this drawing exists between its central horse and the Pale Horse in West's final picture (Pl. 45). In both cases the horses emerge from the background at the same angle, their prancing legs are identically placed, and their heads turn to the right. Did West see the drawing just before he decided to enlarge his picture to its final size? Did he then determine to model his Pale Horse after this ancient example? Possibly, but several features of similarity between the drawing and all of the versions of "Death on the Pale Horse" would seem to indicate that he was familiar with the drawing before he made the first sketch of 1783. For instance, the drawing of the sarcophagus shows figures trampled beneath the central horse, and these figures protect themselves with arms raised in the same position West has used for one of his figures. The horse which rides off at the right of the drawing finds its counterpart in the first apocalyptic rider's horse in West's picture. The similarity is again strongest between the drawing and the final picture, as if West had refreshed his mind by a closer look at the drawing before making his late version.

The most interesting aspect of the Windsor drawing which is carried over into West's pictures is its frieze-like composition. The several versions of "Death on the Pale Horse," while recalling Rubens' spatial effects, tend at the same time to assume a frieze form because the major figures are maintained parallel with the picture plane across its breadth. The classical frieze composition explains a curious spatial and temporal anomaly in West's picture. The text he has illustrated is Revelation, chapter 6, which establishes an interval of time and space between the appearance of each Horseman. Death is the fourth of

75

them to appear, and he has been preceded by the three which West has painted riding off at the right side of the picture. From the text, one would have expected the first three riders to have long since disappeared, and to have ridden off in the same direction taken by Death. Even Dürer's famous print, which shows the Four Horsemen simultaneously, implies that they ride out in the same direction. But in West's picture the first three riders seem to have arrived at the same moment as Death, and, indeed, they appear to be spatially a little behind him. The resulting picture hardly illustrates the biblical passage, but can be best accounted for if West was imitating a classical composition. He has gained immensely in emotional power by including all the Horsemen, but giving Death the dominant position.

The impact of the final picture is considerably heightened by the enlargement of Death and his Pale Horse (Pl. 45) so that they loom huge above the rest of the forms. Such enlargement of the protagonists in a scene is another device of the Dread Manner. Again, in the mad scene from *King Lear* (Pl. 57) West increased the stature of the frenzied king. The effect is rendered plausible by showing the other figures crouching about him; the result is not at all incongruous, because it satisfies the spectator's expectation of tragic grandeur.

In West's Dread Manner the new vehemence of gesture and action was accompanied by facial expressions indicating anguish, surprise, terror, or other strong emotions. West was guided by an innate dramatic sense, and he gauged these facial expressions carefully so that they would be convincing in view of the degree of emotion which any figure might be expected to display. Although verging upon melodrama, he very rarely violated the credibility of any character's facial expression. The faces in his "Conversion of St. Paul" (Pl. 49) are cases in point, for none of them oversteps the bounds of imaginative reality. One of his most intense experiments in conveying strong emotional feeling by facial expression is "Thetis Bringing the Armor to Achilles" (Pl. 53), where the famous wrath of the hero, partially indicated in the tense pose, is chiefly concentrated in his face. Though the effect will not appeal to modern dramatic taste, it can be recognized, nevertheless, as a bold invention within the framework of the Dread Manner.[44]

One more important source for West's figures in his second style must be noticed. He seems to have become obsessed by the "Laocoon" statue. Achilles' pose recalls Laocoon's in the strained position of the legs, and St. Paul (Pl. 49), King Lear (Pl. 57), Diomed (Pl. 58), Cupid (Pl. 60), and the angels in Plates 3 and 62 are all slight variations of the "Laocoon's" pose. West would have seen the original statue in the Vatican and he might have known Girardon's copy of it at Holkham Hall. A full-scale plaster cast was available in the Royal Academy,[45] and West had a small copy in his own house.[46] In one form or another the "Laocoon" was always available for him; nor is it surprising that this great statue, so noted in West's lifetime,[47] would have been the source for some of his most vigorous figures.

The "Laocoon" calls forth an emotional reaction very different from that evoked by the calm figures which influenced West's early works. It elicits a disturbing response by the effect of tensed muscles and struggling forms. Its figures are shown as if in motion instead of in poised, balanced attitudes; its major axis is a diagonal rather than a vertical line, and in place of repose, a restless atmosphere is induced by the varied directions of the gestures and the turn of the heads. That West sought such a prototype indicates the new emotional aims of his Dread Manner.

COMPOSITIONAL DEVICES

So far, vehemence of action, occasional enlargement of major figures, and strong animation of faces have been noticed as elements of West's second style. Now attention may be directed to more general compositional features. The pictures already discussed, and especially "Diomed Stopped by the Lightning of Jupiter" (Pl. 58),[48] show a type of composition essentially different from that of West's earlier works. The calm Raphaelesque system of symmetrical arrangement is no longer frequent, but has been superseded by a diagonal system of apparently receding forms, which recalls the Baroque manner of Rubens. A glance at the source for West's Diomed picture will make his debt to Rubens clear (Pl. 59), and it will be remembered that "Death on the Pale Horse" also showed effects similar to Rubens'. The way had been prepared for this development in West's style by his use of the Bolognese prototypes in his early paintings, but a comparison of his "Ascension" (Pl. 39) with the "Diomed Stopped" will show the difference between early and high Baroque composition, the difference between Carracci and Rubens. Diagonal recession of the forms is far more insistent in the "Diomed Stopped," and the symmetry of the foreground figures has been abandoned. Also abandoned is the foreground depth, so that the main figures are now given a startling prominence. They seem about to burst forth from the canvas surface, since only a minimum pictorial space separates them from the observer. This new immediacy may be seen, too, in the "King Lear" (Pl. 57) where it brings home the powerful emotionalism of the figures. Both Diomed, the furious warrior of the *Iliad*, and Lear, the mad king who feels kinship with the wildness of the storm, have met their match in the power of the elements. Neither of these admirably sublime themes has been treated with the least classical reserve. Instead the imminence of the heroes heightens the impact of their plights upon the observer, sympathetically awakening emotion and arousing associations. Immediacy of the figures becomes a principle of West's "dread" compositions, for the more vividly the subject can be brought to attention, the more suddenly and deeply will the observer's sensibilities be stimulated.

The principle of immediacy was well applied in "The Destruction of the Beast and the False Prophet" (Pl. 56), illustrating Revelation, 19: 11–12. Here the foreground as a distinct, receding plane is omitted, and the eye, introduced at once into the turmoil of dim forms, is engulfed by the dark space.

This picture demonstrates another very important principle of the Dread Manner, the use of obscurity. Burke had advocated obscurity as a major source of the Sublime, and even recommended a certain judicious use of it to painters.[49] Burke meant primarily the obscurity in vision resulting from darkness, but he also implied an admiration for vagueness, a clouding of mental clarity, consequent upon dimmed perception. West's frequent use of large dark areas in his pictures may be seen to correspond with Burke's initial meaning of obscurity, but it is possible that West also attempted to incorporate the second meaning, vagueness, by disregarding clear spatial relationships between objects painted in the heavy shadows. The demons, monsters, and dark powers in this picture are strangely jumbled together so that the eye makes little progress through this part of the composition; their forms are incomplete, and they lack space in which to exist. This same curious deficiency is even more noticeable in the "Omnia Vincit Amor" (Pl. 60), where the figures of Venus and Cupid are well-realized forms

79

in adequate space, but the lion and horse are irrationally crowded together and give the impossible impression of occupying the same space. Though this picture no longer illustrates the "terrible sublime," it retains the influence of Burke's obscurity in the confused forms of the animals. One's natural inclination might be to assume that West has made a blunder in draftsmanship, but this probably does him an injustice, since he usually shows himself capable of adequate drawing. It is probable that he deliberately rejected normal spatial relationships when painting fabulous creatures, like the powers of darkness or allegorical beings. West would seem to have obscured his forms intentionally to achieve the Sublime, adding the obscurity of confusion to that of darkness as appropriate for his Dread Manner.

As a foil to the obscurity of darkness West alternated his dark colors with light tones. "St. Paul Shaking off the Viper" (Pl. 61), illustrating Acts, chapter 28, depends for much of its effectiveness upon the rapid sequence of light and dark areas which displays the agitated poses of its figures, setting each off sharply against the next. As Burke said, "A quick transition from light to darkness, and from darkness to light has a yet greater effect than lightning."[50] All of the pictures in the Dread Manner, which have been examined here, show this alternation of darks and lights, and the subtle tonal gradations of West's earlier works are gone. The principle of abrupt tonal contrasts may be deduced, then, as an essential element of his "dread" compositional methods. West inclined towards the use of broad silhouettes, either of light or dark tone, which were relieved against a background of contrasting tone. This simple tonal contrast can be seen well in "Elijah Convincing the False Prophets of Baol," (Pl. 62) illustrating I Kings, chapter 18, where the modeling of forms is minimized and a broad effect is suggested by the interplay of dark and light silhouettes.

In the Dread Manner West's coloring was not bright. Browns predominate in these pictures, because the Sublime was found best in whatever was dark and gloomy.[51] A new assurance of execution is seen in West's work during this phase. Even his handling of paint acquired new breadth. Whereas the earlier works had been very smoothly painted, the smoothness itself being part of his classicizing perfectionism, the pictures in the Dread Manner show a rough, broad application; often the separate touches are left unblended. This rough effect was perfectly consonant with Burke's Sublime, for, as Burke wrote, "beauty should be smooth and polished; the great, rugged and negligent."[52] This seems a fair description of West's two manners.

The Dread Manner operated within a broadly defined classicism, which neither Burke nor West would abandon. West did not sacrifice the basic moral intention and didactic aim of classicism, for his "dread" pictures could elevate and purge the emotions. Moreover, as has been shown, West continued to draw inspiration from the art of classical antiquity. In these ways he preserved throughout the Dread Manner the classicist's conviction that ancient art should supply the models for current works. His second style was not evolved in revolt against classicism, rather it contributed materially to the traditional body of artistic criteria by extending the premise that a picture should be emotionally moving.

CHAPTER FOUR

THE PATHETIC STYLE

———— ✳ ————

FROM THE TERRIBLE SUBLIME
TO THE PATHETIC

As a background for West's last style of painting, it will be helpful to consider the eighteenth-century meaning of the word Pathetic. This term was allied with the Sublime, and described whatever was strongly stimulating to the emotions. Burke's "terrible sublime" was fully pathetic in that it depended upon an experience of the strongest emotions, but the question might be raised whether Burke had defined sublimity justly, or whether he had not merely analyzed a state of strong emotional disturbance. The validity of Burke's theory was seriously compromised by the publication of Richard Payne Knight's *Principles of Taste* in 1805, which must have been widely read, since it ran into four editions within four years.[1] Knight quoted Longinus' ancient treatise *On the Sublime* to show that Burke had violated the most fundamental principle of sublimity: ". . . the effect of the sublime is *to lift up the soul; to exalt it into ecstacy . . . wherefore, the passions of grief, sorrow, fear, &c. are incapable of any sublime expression; or of produc-*

ing any sublime effect."[2] So Burke's equation of sublimity with the emotion of fear was held to be essentially misleading, and Knight complained: "... for the word *sublime*, both according to its use and etymology, must signify *high* or *exalted*; and, if an individual choose, that in his writings, it should signify *terrible*, he only involves his meaning in a confusion of terms, which naturally leads to a confusion of ideas."[3]

Knight granted that a terrifying object might be considered sublime, but he refused to believe that terror was the cause of any elevating feelings; terror could induce only feelings of inferiority, because it was a self-centered emotion: "No merely selfish sorrow or affliction, how justly and eloquently soever expressed, can ever be pathetic in fiction; because it can never be, in any degree, sublime; but must always exhibit more of the weaknesses than the energies of the mind."[4]

Moreover, Knight objected that the fictions of poetry, drama, or painting could not cause terror, because they never really deceive the spectator. An observer's admiration was stirred, not by sympathetically engendered fears, but by sympathy with *power*, by the sight of great exertions, and "energies of the mind," which a subject would display when under the stress of terror. In this way the struggles of gladiators, bullfighters, and boxers could become admirable spectacles because the fighters were goaded by fear to perform extraordinary feats of skill and courage. The plight of a tragic hero, or heroine, would also provoke a display of what Knight called "energetic passions," which he believed essential for moving the spectator's emotions. As he said, "All sympathies, excited by just and appropriate expression of energetic passion; whether they be of the tender or violent kind, are alike sublime; as they all tend to expand and elevate the mind; and fill it with those enthusiastic raptures, which Longinus justly states to be the true feelings of sublimity. Hence that author cites instances of sublime from the tenderest odes of love, as well as from the most terrific images of war; and with equal propriety. . . ."[5]

Knight believed the energetic passions, which art must imitate, might be "furious and impetuous" or "mild and gentle," but they had to be "decisive," more enthusiastic than rational. If they lacked specific character, they would not be clearly recognized, and when portrayed in a work of art they would not enlist an observer's sympathy. The emotions most desirable for an artist's imitation had to be strong, such as "the sentiments of heroism, fortitude, constancy, or tenderness," which "produce the interest; and awaken all the exquisite and delightful thrills of sympathy."[6] But besides these elevating passions, "hatred and malignity" were strongly affecting in a drama or a painted scene. Hatred was decidedly an energetic passion: ". . . and, consequently, well adapted to excite sentiments and expressions of great and enthusiastic force and vigor; with which we sympathize . . . [though] not with the passion itself. . . ."[7] Knight's ultimate hope was that a work of art might exhibit a rich variety of passions: ". . . an interesting struggle of contending affections; from which emanate the most striking flashes of glowing, pathetic, sublime and vigorous sentiment; with all which we sympathize, in proportion to the truth, spirit, and energy, with which they are expressed."[8]

By imitating the outward appearances of figures under the stress of various emotions art becomes "pathetic." Knight used this term in its eighteenth-century sense, not merely implying pitiful, as it does today, but meaning whatever could strongly induce sentimental reactions. He shaded the meaning to indicate passions of a generally tender nature, while he associated the word sublime with more vigorous emotions, "exalted or enthusiastic passions." But in art he felt the Sublime and the Pathetic merged, for, "In all the fictions, either of poetry or imitative art, there can be nothing truly pathetic, unless it be, at the same time, in some degree, sublime . . . a display of vigor, as well as tenderness and sensibility of mind."[9]

The consequence of this theory for painting was the use of both heroically elevating and tender subjects, with a vigorous, in fact, rather self-conscious, delineation of "energetic passions" in the painted gestures and faces.

Whether West read Knight's *Principles of Taste* cannot be determined, but he was acquainted with the author,[10] and probably knew his ideas. Knight, in turn, knew West's painting, and he described "The Death of General Wolfe" as one "of the most interesting and affecting pictures, that the art has ever produced."[11] So there are reasons to assume a degree of familiarity between West and Knight. At any rate, Knight's *Principles of Taste* presents a theory which is amply illustrated in West's late works, and West's turn to a style aptly called "pathetic" corresponds approximately in time with the publication of Knight's opinions in 1805.

WEST'S SENTIMENTAL ESSAY

In the last fifteen years of his career West developed a style of painting which can be described best by the word pathetic, because his aim was to provoke various emotions strongly in the observer's mind. While the Dread Manner had been similarly emotive in stirring strong feelings, it had been limited to arousing emotions of astonishment and terror. The last, or Pathetic Style, sought to extend the range of emotions desirable in art to include noble and tender feelings.

Emotional responses could be keenly aroused by a picture if the painter successfully imitated the appearance of strong emotions in his "actors." The idea of representing the passions by gestures and facial expressions was part of the traditional practice of art, but it received new impetus from the eighteenth-century theories of associative and sympathetic assimilation of emotions by the spectator. If the artist projected himself imaginatively into the feelings of the character he was portraying, in turn the observer was believed able to extract those feelings sympathetically from the painted figures. In "pathetic" pictures, then, one must expect to find figures under the strain of energetic passions, either tempestuous or tender.

In the earlier chapters West's choice of themes and the style of his figures have been discussed separately, but it will be best to study his late subjects and figure types together, because the emotions which the figures display become the real themes of his pictures. In the Pathetic Style a biblical picture, for instance "Christ Healing the Sick in the Temple" (Pl. 4), is no longer simply an illustration of that event, but it has become the vehicle for a complex display of varied emotions. Its figures demonstrate a wide range of sentiments, their faces and gestures show expressions varying from disbelief in Christ's power, through doubt and hope, to expectation and calm assurance. The whole picture presents "an interesting struggle of contending affections," as Knight had suggested a picture at its best should. So in the following discussion West's subjects and emotive figures will be examined simultaneously.

The sources of West's subject matter in his late period remained the same as before, mythological, historical, biblical, and literary, but now he chose themes to reveal mild and elevating sentiments, such as reverence, respect, sympathy, and love. For instance, although the Bible remained a favorite source, he no longer illustrated its tense, wonder-inducing passages, but sought out stories which excited gentle religious feeling, as in the "Christ Healing." The 1817 version of "Death on the Pale Horse" (Pl. 45) was exceptional in carrying on the theme of the terrible sublime, but it must be noted that the apocalyptic Horsemen would have been as acceptable to Knight's theory as to Burke's. While both would have seen it as terrifying, Knight could have admired the omnipotence of the deadly riders, finding their power (not the terror they caused) the source of their sublimity. One must not imagine that West took a deliberate stand against the terrible sublime in his latter years, for he seems to have recognized it as a distinct genre of sublimity. However, it may be said that his dominant interest shifted from themes of terror to themes involving gentler emotions. Confirmation of this change in his taste can be seen in his late interpretation of "The Conversion of St. Paul" (Pl. 63) when it is compared with his earlier version (Pl. 49). In this case the theme is even the same, but the picture of 1812 shows how the subject, which was treated in the Dread Manner in 1786, could be reinterpreted in the Pathetic Style. Gestures of wonder and astonishment are still present, but the earlier excitement and turmoil has been replaced by an air of reverent awe. The composition has become calm, the figures are spread, frieze-like, across the surface, and a serene Poussinesque landscape added behind them. The figure style in the late version differs from the types of the Dread Manner, most obviously by showing the figures in more relaxed poses; there is less twisting, turning, and gesturing. Also, the late figures are more smoothly painted; the rugged effect of West's "dread" handling is superseded by more softly modeled forms. This is true of nearly all of West's late figures, only in sketches of relatively small size is the rough brush work still noticeable.

In his late style West returned to his early interest in the noble theme of the hero, capitalizing particularly on its sentimental potentialities. In a vast canvas he commemorated "The Death of Lord Nelson" (Pl. 64), a theme combining patriotic enthusiasm for the nation's great naval hero with feelings of commiseration for his death. The picture shows innumerable figures swarming over the deck and rigging of the *Victory* to pay homage to their dying leader. While West had frequently painted the theme of a hero's death in his early days, he never did it in the Dread Manner. Knight's admiration for "The Death of General Wolfe" has been mentioned, and probably it is no accident that West determined to repeat his earlier success. He linked the themes of Wolfe and Nelson together in his own mind, for he told Farington: "Wolfe must not die like a common Soldier under a Bush; neither should Nelson be represented dying in the gloomy hold of a Ship, like a sick man in a Prison Hole.—To move the mind there should be a spectacle presented to raise & warm the mind, & all shd. be proportioned to the highest idea conceived of the Hero. No Boy, sd. West, wd. be animated by a representation of Nelson dying like an ordinary man, His feelings must be roused & His mind inflamed by a scene great & extraordinary. A mere matter of fact will never produce this effect."[12]

In spite of this statement, West tried showing the death of Nelson "in the gloomy hold of a ship," as may be seen in his picture of 1808 (Pl. 65). It is not a very successful picture with its too obvious emotionalism, but it assumes interest as an essay in the Pathetic Style, for here are "energetic passions" strongly shown. It is clearly less fortunate than the version of three years later, the large exhibition piece, now in Liverpool (Pl. 64). Here the primary concern is sublimity, defined as "a spectacle to raise and warm the mind . . . proportionate to the highest idea of the Hero." The Pathetic also plays its part: "feelings must be roused . . . mind influenced by a scene great and extraordinary." But Burke's requisite terror is omitted. Conceived in humanly moving terms, the picture shows the concern of Nelson's men at the moment he is fatally wounded, rather than the scene of his actual death, which took place below deck. In this way the grand spectacle is sustained. West must have been gratified at the pathetic power of his picture, for when men viewed it they were so moved that they reverently removed their hats.[13]

In another picture West painted Nelson's death as a classical allegory of immortality, "The Apotheosis of Nelson" (Pl. 66). A gigantic Neptune rises from the sea to lift Nelson into the arms of Britannia, who "sits in shaded gloom, as expressive of that deep regret which overwhelmed the United Kingdom. . . ."[14] The picture is particularly important, because it indicates the strong classical sympathies West still maintained, and shows how these might include such "pathetic" sentiments as respect and sorrow.

The theme of human sympathy, as it merged into pity, often engaged West's attention. To be sure, Knight had been very skeptical about pity, feeling that it rarely could elevate the observer's mind. Only if the object of one's pity were in genuinely dire circumstances, and only if his predicament were manfully borne with restraint, could pity "melt the mind to love," and so become pathetic.[15] It is exactly this definition of pity's role in producing emotive effects which is filled by West's "Belisarius and the Boy" (Pl. 68).[16] Justinian's great general is shown in his old age, and, as a blind and beggared outcast, he excites the commiseration of a youth who knew the tales of his former glory. Belisarius' plight was genuinely pitiful, and, as may be seen, West pictured him suffering it bravely, even seeming to reassure the boy by placing a hand upon his shoulder. So conceived, Belisarius is ripe to "melt the heart" by stirring admiration mixed with the pity he must arouse. The boy in the picture has been posed to convey this blend of emotions directly to the spectator, to whom he turns. His face and gesture eloquently attest his conflicting emotions, in which pity seems dominant. However, one is equally expected to consider Belisarius himself, and the figure is eminently pathetic in both modern and eighteenth-century senses. It is again clear that the figures are the emotive agents in West's late paintings. There is little effort to render the backgrounds expressive of the story's mood, as was the case in his Dread Manner. The backgrounds have become simply tasteful adjuncts to the figures which crowd the canvases, filling them with emotive types.

When in this last phase themes were chosen from antiquity, West no longer favored the legends of terrible conflict, but was inclined towards ancient tales of love. "Cupid and Psyche" (Pl. 69) is a good illustration of his interest in Knight's "pathetic expression." It is indicative of the new stress upon the softer sentiments, the feelings Burke had not felt to be sublime but only beautiful. The picture, indeed, is almost compatible with Burke's ideas on beauty, which he conceived to be grounded in love. But differentiating it from Burke's notion of love as pleasurably relaxing, is the concentrated intensity of expression on the faces, especially in the eyes. West has shown love as an "energetic," even dominant passion, and so he has reflected Knight's principles. By intensifying the facial expressions West raised love, from a source of beauty only, to become an agent of the Pathetic and Sublime.

To show love as a dominant emotion entailed a very overt expression of sentiment in the actions and in the enraptured faces. This tendency to "overact" will be seen as characteristic of most of West's late pictures. Such was not the case in the earlier Dread Manner, where terror was the predominant emotion and gave adequate motivation for West's forceful drawing of gestures and facial expressions. Some of the late works, the "Christ Rejected" (Pl. 70) for example, contain faces and figures which are notably apt for their emotional expressiveness, but even here some expressions seem unnaturally forced. West probably felt that the gentle emotions, such as reverence, sympathy, pity, and love, needed to be overdrawn, or their mild effects would be lost. To modern eyes his overemphasized emotionalism seems unfortunately sentimental. Such a reaction is almost inescapable today, but in the light of Knight's demand for emotive expression, it will be realized that West's intention was not to popularize his pictures by giving them obvious sentimental appeal. He hoped to move his spectators profoundly, and there can be no doubt of his sincerity. His works were true to the ideals of a period when the psychological effects of art were understood by the postulates of mental association and sympathetic assimilation, and when the didactic end of art was still maintained by classical principles.

Direct prototypes in West's Pathetic or Emotive Style are far less evident than in his earlier works because of a growing assurance. He became more freely inventive in his late paintings, though still confining himself chiefly to gestures and poses of the classical tradition. His confidence in his own ability to design figures within the limits of classicizing taste must have increased, since it is no longer possible to trace his figures directly from ancient, Renaissance, or Baroque works.

His new freedom in imitation may be seen in the "Christ Healing the Sick" (Pl. 4). Probably he consulted Rembrandt's "Hundred Guilder Print" for its treatment of the same theme and he may have drawn from it the general idea of a majestic, standing Christ with a recumbent invalid brought before Him. The mother holding a sick child, towards whom Christ's right hand points, is another link between the pictures, but all the details of West's version are quite independently developed. Nor do they give the impression of being so much imitated from other sources as devised by West for their special roles in the scene.

In view of his apparent independence, it is interesting to find that West himself claimed a source for this picture and for his "Christ Rejected" (Pl. 70) in the Elgin marbles.[17] As an examination of these pictures will show, there is no case of direct borrowing from any of the Elgin sculptures, so one must conclude that West meant he had generally improved his style by studying the Phidian examples, and perhaps felt he had recaptured their spirit in these two paintings. The Elgin marbles represented for him "sublime specimens of the purest sculpture,"[18] while, at the same time, he was impressed by their vigorous naturalism. He wrote of the "Theseus," and the "Ilisus," and of some of the best metopes, "The close imitation of nature visible in these Figures, adds an excellence to them which words are incapable of describing. . . ."[19] These opinions perfectly express the eighteenth-century attitude towards the best ancient works. Such sculptures appeared both sublime and natural, noble and realistic. West did not distinguish the Phidian works sharply from his former Hellenistic and Roman favorites, but rather claimed that "the same powers are visible in the Barberini Sleeping Faun."[20] In his Discourse of 1811, he followed his praise of Lord Elgin's collection with equal praise for the "Apollo Belvedere," the "Medici Venus," the "Laocoon," and the "Dying Gaul."[21] He had not modern scholarship to guide his taste and could depend upon little more than his own observations and preference. If one remembers that Phidian art together with later Greek and Roman works all presented to West and his contemporaries the same vision of ideal nature, one may feel that the claim of Phidian inspiration in the "Christ Healing" and "Christ Rejected" was justified. The figures in these paintings are full of life and sentiment in their facial expressions and gestures, while at the same time their types are idealized. This blend of real and ideal nature was seen in the works from antiquity, and West's figures fulfilled this conception of ancient art.

Besides this classicism in West's late painting, the "Christ Rejected" (Pl. 70) reveals a strong affinity with Poussin's art, for a series of analogies link it with Poussin's "Worship of the Golden Calf" (Pl. 72).[22] While these similarities of composition and detail might be circumstantial if taken individually, their combined evidence is fairly conclusive in indicating an actual source for West's picture. As is often the case in West's borrowing, there is an underlying identity of theme; in this instance both pictures deal with a sacrilegious situation. Both compositions center upon a figure with outstretched arms. The whole right-hand, triangular grouping of figures is common to both compositions, and a crowd of figures presses in towards the center of both pictures, forming a frieze in the middle distance. Points of more detailed correspondence are offered by the bare shoulder of West's executioner and the bare back of Poussin's elderly male dancer, compositionally in the same place. The attitude of West's Magdalen finds its echo in the kneeling, pointing woman of Poussin's picture, and the gesture of remonstrance from a centurion at the extreme left of West's picture parallels the agitation of Moses as he comes down the mountain in Poussin's painting. Finally, the odd gesture of the old man who holds up his two hands before Barabbas, at the right of West's picture, finds a parallel in the similarly placed, upraised hands of Poussin's work.

West's admiration for Poussin is frequently reflected in his late works. It is seen, for example, in the late "Conversion of St. Paul" (Pl. 63), where Poussin's Arcadian landscape setting, with its trees and hills arranged like receding scenic flats, is vividly recalled, and the figures, like Poussin's, are introduced in near and distant friezes across the width of the picture.

In many ways West's late style returned to the pictorial forms that had characterized his early pictures. The spiritual affinity with Phidian art, absorbed from his study of the Elgin marbles, and the influence of Poussin, both of which dominated his Pathetic Style, parallel his earlier fondness for serene classical work and for Raphael's more restrained pictures. But in the Pathetic Style there was also a source in external nature as well as in tradition. In his mature painting of facial expression and eloquent gesture, which are very apt in the "Christ Rejected," there is a strong suggestion that West studied people about him with an eye for catching their emotions, reflected in their faces, attitudes, and actions.

EMOTIVE COMPOSITION

West's outstanding work in "pathetic" expression was his large canvas, "Christ Rejected" (Pl. 70), completed in 1814. In the center the Jewish high priest, Caiaphas, denounces Christ as a blasphemer before a vast crowd, some of whom are Christ's sympathizers, while others are his enemies. A very original conception of the theme has allowed West to introduce an extraordinary range of emotions, completely satisfying the needs of his Pathetic Style. These emotions play from the stolid indifference of the executioners through Mary's grief, from Pilate's indecision to the frenzied rage of Caiaphas. Each of the main figures has been imagined under the stress of some powerful feeling, of which the high priest's hatred appears the strongest. Farington's *Diary* tells how West believed he had "conquered His greatest difficulty in having painted the *High Priest* giving Him the whole force of what He had in His mind of that character."[23] The villainous Caiaphas has stolen attention from all the other figures, but his prominence is understandable in the light of Knight's theories; Caiaphas' fury is not only "pathetically moving," but sublimely emotive. As Knight said, "Not only love, however, but its opposite, hatred and malignity, may be sublime in poetry; as that of Shylock, in some scenes of Shakspeare, unquestionably is: not that malignity is a sublime passion: but that, in strong and powerful minds, such as that of Shylock is feigned to be, it is an energetic one; and, consequently, well adapted to excite sentiments and expressions of great and enthusiastic force and vigour...."[24] Caiaphas does not rend his garments, as he was said to have in the biblical text (Matt. 26: 65), but West was

96

evidently less concerned with factual illustration than with "giving supernatural force and energy to every image and expression . . . to raise the mind above the contemplation of ordinary nature."[25]

The way West has arranged the varied emotions of the other figures around Caiaphas was graphically demonstrated in a pamphlet circulated in 1830 when "Christ Rejected" was exhibited at Independence Hall in Philadelphia.[26] A diagram in the pamphlet (Pl. 71) describes the range of feelings West has painted: Caiaphas in "the strongest paroxysm of envy and rage," Christ showing "innocence and meekness," the Magdalen exhibiting "the warmest expression of fear, compassion, and zeal," and many more are indicated. Lines on the diagram link the various emotions by analogy, sympathy, opposition, or contrast, and so indicate a kind of emotive composition created by the balance or contrast of sentiments. West attempted to move the spectators by exciting both their sympathies and antipathies towards the painted actors in his drama, treating his picture as if it were a dramatic production. Even the villains, however, were ennobled by the strength of their convictions, so that the whole performance sustains the elevated mood of ancient tragedy. By portraying so clearly mutually analogous and contrary emotions, the "Christ Rejected" demonstrates a new kind of pictorial composition which West contrived in his late works. It is a "pathetic," or emotive type of composition, in which the pictorial structure is determined by the calculated arrangement of various figures, to which the spectator reacts emotionally. It is a kind of composition which may be found in many of West's late works in the Pathetic Style, though usually in less concentrated form. "Belisarius and the Boy" exhibited harmonious feelings experienced by its two figures; "Christ Healing" revealed both sympathetic and antagonistic sentiments, and was composed as an interplay of emotions.

The complex display of varied sentiments in West's emotive composition was essentially a response to the eighteenth-century belief that one reacted to a work of art by sympathetic imagination. From the earlier discussion of critical trends in this period, it may be recalled that sympathy was believed to be the chief agent of esthetic perception. Mental associations might give rise to esthetic experience, or they might build that knowledge, which with intuitive "sensibility," united to form sympathy.[27] Significantly, "Christ Rejected" almost surely reflects both the psychologies of mental association and of sympathetic assimilation. The latter is amply attested by West's emotive composition, which makes its varied appeal through one's sympathies. But the picture also reveals a kind of associative composition, which sprang from West's peculiar eclecticism, and must be analyzed now.

TRADITIONAL ICONOGRAPHY AND ASSOCIATIVE COMPOSITION

West's practice of using traditional iconographic schemes of composition for new subjects is demonstrated well in the "Christ Rejected" (Pl. 70), for here he combined iconographic elements from three separate episodes of Christ's Passion, two of which were drawn from established pictorial traditions. The actual text for Christ's rejection (Matt. 26: 57–69) concerns only the figures of Christ, the high priest Caiaphas, some scribes and elders of the temple, and perhaps some of

Christ's captors. It took place in an inner room of Caiaphas' house. But in painting his picture West enlarged upon the event by including the happenings of the following day (Matt. 27: 1–27), showing Pilate and Barabbas in the same scene.[28] For this reason he has used the traditional iconography of the *Ecce Homo* theme, in which Christ is shown to the people, while Pilate points to him. However, the people whom West has painted are not the angry crowd which preferred Barabbas, but the friends and followers of Christ, and they are painted in attitudes which recall the traditional Crucifixion iconography. So it is that Mary Magdalen kneels in the center foreground, in a position and pose which she frequently assumes in pictures of the Crucifixion. St. John supports the Virgin Mary, who is about to swoon, and the Good Centurion is included; both are features in the traditional pictures of Christ's death upon the cross. The very form of the cross itself is suggested by the outstretched arms of the high priest and the upraised arm of the figure behind him. Such close analogies with Crucifixion iconography can hardly be coincidental, and the conclusion is inevitable that West added these elements of the *Ecce Homo* and Crucifixion themes to extend the significance of his picture. In the violence of Caiaphas' denouncement of Christ one is intended to read the coming trial and ultimate sacrifice of Christ.[29] In this light West's eclecticism assumes new meaning, for he has used his knowledge of traditional forms to amplify the expressiveness of his work. The term "associative composition" might conveniently be applied to this ingenious system of imitation, in which one is led to associate the emotional overtones of a traditional iconography with an entirely new theme. In view of the eighteenth-century psychology of associationism, discussed in Chapter III, West's system of composing by associating together a chain of episodes is particularly significant, indicating his interest in advanced critical thought.

An explanation for the persistence of several traditional types of iconography which run throughout West's work may be found in his associative composition. One of his favorite schemes was that of the Deposition, or descent from the cross.[30] In pictures of this theme, Christ's body is shown in a tortured attitude of intense suffering, and about it cluster many who support or lament over Him. Such a grouping occurs in West's "Death of General Wolfe" (Pl. 5), and his intention was surely to re-enforce the poignancy of the moment by allusion to the conventional representation of Christ's deposition from the cross.[31]

Furthermore, it should be noticed that the iconography of the Crucifixion is called to mind in the "Death of General Wolfe" by the grieving soldier at the extreme right. His clasped hands conform to a traditional attitude assumed by the figure of St. John at the foot of the cross.[32] Also the group at the left, behind the seated Indian, recalls the figures shown frequently surrounding the Virgin in Crucifixion pictures. Even the Virgin's traditional swooning attitude is echoed by the tallest soldier in West's group, the figure leaning backward, with hand on chest, as if overcome by emotion.

The traditional composition of the Passion scenes clearly occurred to West again when he came to commemorate the passing of another national hero, Lord Nelson. In both the pictures of the death and in the apotheosis of Nelson (Plates 64–66) the limp body is posed like that of Christ in many Deposition, Lamentation, or Entombment scenes. The observer's awareness of Nelson's sacrifice is thus heightened, as again West's eclecticism underlines a symbolic meaning.

Madonna compositions, too, affected West's way of visualizing his pictures. The *tondo* showing the artist's wife and child (Pl. 73) is surely related to Raphael's "Madonna della Sedia" in the Uffizi Gallery, of which West owned a small copy.[33] In "Agrippina Mourning" (Pl. 25) West unquestionably had in mind the tradition of the Christ Child and the young St. John the Baptist playing together at the Virgin's knee, a favorite arrangement of countless Madonna pictures (cf. Raphael's "Madonna del Cardelino").[34]

The Christian paintings of the Crucifixion, Deposition, and the Madonna were the chief sources for West's associative composition, probably because these were the scenes with most familiar connotations, and with iconographic arrangements most adaptable to new contexts. Besides these Christian traditions, West borrowed schemes from seventeenth-century painting to aid in visualizing his pictures. For example "The Appeal to Coriolanus" (Pl. 23) draws extensively upon the traditional ancient camp scenes like Le Brun's "Tent of Darius," which West could have known from an engraving.[35] But such subjects had not the familiar aspects of the Christian themes with their strong emotional appeal, so that when West used them it was less for their associational values than as aids in composing.

The classical battle scene, however, was more stirring, and West put its elements—rearing horses, trampled victims, and armed men— to use in "Death on the Pale Horse" (Pl. 45).[36]

From these examples of general affinity between West's pictures and earlier iconographic traditions, his reasons for allegiance to the powerfully dramatic tradition of Humanistic art are evident. He not only sought to keep alive the classical tradition, but also used it to strengthen the emotional impact of his work. He did not actually copy earlier compositions, but imitated them with the full license which the eighteenth-century meaning of imitation allowed him. Frequently he adapted traditional forms cleverly to new subjects, capitalizing upon their traditional associations to contribute power to his own conceptions. His eclecticism, therefore, not only maintained the classical style and ideals, but also added a new expressive potentiality, which no other painter exploited as fully as did West.

CONCLUSION

The purpose of this study has been to invite the reader to consider West's paintings in relation to eighteenth-century critical expectations, and to see how successfully he realized the esthetic aims of his age.

Classicizing idealism was the esthetic which West maintained, but he enlarged its scope to accommodate new critical demands for emotional and sentimental qualities. Ingeniously he molded traditional artistic conventions, at first, to approximate the effects of ancient sculpture and so to incorporate that magic sublimity which he and his contemporaries found in antique marbles. Next, his style sought a new sublimity by expressing sensations of infinity, power, and fear. Finally, he strove to move his spectators' sentiments by pathetic human dramas, and contrived new forms of pictorial composition to heighten associational and emotional responses. When such achievements are considered, West appears as a versatile master, who pointed the way to both Neoclassical and Romantic art.

APPENDIX, NOTES,
BIBLIOGRAPHY,
INDEX

APPENDIX

—————————— ✳ ——————————

WEST ON COLORING

In 1803 West discussed with George III "the Philosophy of Colours to shew that all combinations are derived from the Prismatick colours."[1] Again in 1817 Lawrence heard West speak extempore for half an hour in the Academy on the use of colors, and was surprised at his eloquence. Farington reported Lawrence's account of the event: "The Principal point He attempted to prove was That The *Order of Colours in a Rainbow*, is the true arrangement in an Historical picture – viz: exhibiting the warm & brilliant colours in a picture where the principal light falls & the *cool colours* in the shade; also that as an accompanying reflection, a weaker rainbow often accompanies the more powerful rainbow, so it may be advisable to repeat the same colours in another part of the Picture to act as *second* to the superior display."[2] West went on to say that while Raphael had not painted in this way in the Vatican frescoes, the tapestry Cartoons showed the rainbow hues perfectly. Titian, he said, had not learned to color like this until he was seventy-five.[3]

West's color theory was not new when either George III or Sir Thomas Lawrence heard it, for he had given it in detail in his Discourse of 1797. In that lecture, after the discussion of light and shade illuminating a ball with subtle gradations of tone, he went on to say: "You will find that this experiment will instruct you, not only in the principles of light and shade, but also of colours; for that there is a corresponding hue with

105

respect to colours is not to be disputed. In order to demonstrate this, place in the ball which you have illuminated, the prismatic colours, suiting their hues to those of the tints. Yellow will answer to the focus of illumination, and the other secondary and primary hues will fall into their proper places. Hence on the enlightened side of a group or figure, you may lay yellow, orange, red, and then violet, but never on the side where the light recedes.[4] On that side must come the other prismatic colours in their natural order. Yellow must pass to green, the green to blue, and the blue to purple. The primary colours of yellow, orange, and red are the warm colours, and belong to the illuminated side of objects; the violet is the intermediate, and the green, blue, and purple are the cold colours, and belong to the retiring parts of your composition.

"On the same principle, and in the same order, must be placed the tints which compose the fleshy bodies of men and women, but so blended with each other, as to give the softness appropriate to the luminous quality and texture of flesh; paying attention, at the same time, to reflections on its surface from other objects, and to its participation of their colours. The latter is a distinct circumstance arising from accident."[5]

West concluded with the advice to study the coloring of Titian, Correggio, Rubens, and Van Dyck, thus admitting the ultimate Venetian inspiration of his theory.[6]

It is amusing to compare the exposition of flesh painting given above with what Farington reported West was actually doing in 1808: ". . . mixing *Ultramarine with his White* so that it should make a part of *every tint*, & by using *Indian Red* only to give warmth, & black in His shadows. – With these colours only He painted His flesh & *when finished*, made use of *warm glazing colours* which [with] the cool, pure colours, produced the most charming *effect*. – He would never use *yellow* in painting His flesh."[7] Like Reynolds, West may have been experimenting in his technique when Farington observed him.[8] He was fascinated by the coloring of Renaissance and Baroque masters, and on numerous occasions analyzed their techniques, showing a special interest in Titian and Rembrandt. To Lawrence and Farington, West spoke of Titian's "Bacchus and Ariadne": "West said it was painted when Titian was abt. 50 years of age, & full of *Giorgione's* feeling of colour. – At a later period Titian aimed more at grandeur & character, but at this period His mind was occupied by a desire to produce the utmost splendour of colouring. – He traced out the . . . ground of bright yellow, glazed down to a

106

tone to suit the intended colour of his picture. But the whole *from the beginning* was worked with *thin colours*, through which the *light within* as He called it, proceeding from the first ground, gave the lustre which was so extraordinary."[9] Again, on seeing Rembrandt's "Woman Taken in Adultery," now in the London National Gallery, West called it "in its way the finest piece of Art in the world," and analyzed its technique in detail.[10] His statements may or may not be correct, but they show his complete knowledge of the possibilities in a glazing technique. He was fully aware of the subtleties of warm and cool colors which could be achieved with oil glazes over a luminous underpainting.

Whether West practiced what he preached is questionable, for his works are rarely notable for their coloring.[11] The most telling aspect of West's color theory was his correlation of color with modeling, and hence, with volume. This is apparent in his suggested experiment of placing the spectrum colors within the illuminated ball. In making this suggestion, he rationalized the practice of the great colorists. That Titian or Rubens could not have thought in terms of Newton's spectrum (published 1672) is inessential. What counts in West's theory is that color and form are unified, being conceived simultaneously by the painter as a variety of hues in different planes. West's color theory was an original contribution, foreshadowing the later interest in color taken by Delacroix, the Impressionists, the Neo-Impressionists, and Cézanne, as well as by nineteenth-century scientists.[12] It differed from these later investigations in being essentially part of a rational-idealist system. West attempted to set a norm (the rainbow hues) for the history painter to follow.

NOTES

—————————— ✵ ——————————

INTRODUCTION

1. The standard biography of West is John Galt, *The Life, Studies, and Works of Benjamin West, Esq., President of the Royal Academy of London, Composed from Materials Furnished by Himself* (London, 1820). This is in two parts, the first having appeared in 1816 published at Philadelphia and dealing with his life prior to his arrival in England. A second edition of this was issued in 1817.

In a letter owned by the Historical Society of Pennsylvania West wrote to Joseph Farington, February 3, 1813, that two reliable biographies had been published, one by Mr. Knight, Stationer, Windsor St., and one of 1805 by Richard Philips, St. Paul's Church Yard.

Next in authority to these accounts is William Dunlap's in *A History of the Rise and Progress of the Arts of Design in the United States* (Boston, 1918), I, 32–109 (first published 1834). The most recent account of West's whole career is in James T. Flexner, *America's Old Masters* (New York, 1939), pp. 19–97. More recent articles will be noted below.

2. William Sawitzky, "The American Work of Benjamin West," *PMHB*, LXII (1938), 433–62.

3. James T. Flexner, "Benjamin West's American Neo-Classicism," *The New-York Historical Society Quarterly*, XXXVI (1952), 5–41.

4. The following list of West's pupils is given in Joseph T. A. Burke, "A Biographical and Critical Study of Benjamin West, 1738–1792" (M.A. thesis, Yale University, 1937), p. 104: M. Pratt, C. W. Peale, J. Wright, J. S. Copley, S. F. B. Morse, G. Stuart, W. Dunlap, J. Trumbull, R. Fulton, T. Sully, R. Earl.

J. H. Pleasants ("George William West, a Baltimore Student of Benjamin West," *Art in America*, XXXVII [1949], 7ff.) adds E. G. Malbone, M. Brown, G. W. West. To these A. Delanoy, Jr., John Green, and W. Allston can be added.

5. Characteristic of praise lavished on West are the lines in Joel Barlow's *The Vision of Columbus* (Baltimore, 1814) on page 207: "His sovereign hand creates impassion'd forms . . . and boldly bursts the former bounds of art." Barlow's enthusiasm might have been occasioned by patriotism, but this view was shared by Englishmen of taste, especially William Hayley, Sir George Beaumont, Sir Martin Archer Shee, and Thomas Lawrence. William Hazlitt was the first to turn against West in print, articles appearing in *The Champion* (London), June 25 and October 1, 1814. Byron made a cruel jibe in *The Curse of Minerva*: "Meantime the flattering feeble dotard West, / Europe's worst dauber, and poor Britain's best, / With palsied hand shall turn each model o'er, / And own himself an infant of fourscore." See *The Complete Works of Lord Byron*, ed. J. W. Lake (Paris, 1825), VII, 85. But it should be remembered that Byron was furious with West, because West had furthered Lord Elgin's plan to sell the Parthenon sculptures to the English government instead of returning them to Greece as Byron wished.

6. Jean Locquin, "La Part de l'Influence Anglaise dans l'Orientation Néo-Classique de la Peinture Française entre 1750 et 1780," *Actes du Congrès d'Histoire de l'Art*, II (1921), 391–402.

7. Sidney Fiske Kimball, "Benjamin West au Salon de 1802," *Gazette des Beaux-Arts*, ser. 6, VII (1932), 403–10.

8. This has been usually dated *ca.* 1771, but it is mentioned as already well known in a letter of March 30, 1770, written by Richard Cumberland to advise George Romney about pictures to be exhibited in that year. Therefore, it is probable that West's "Death of General Wolfe" had been exhibited the previous year. The letter is quoted in Arthur B. Chamberlain, *George Romney* (New York, 1910), p. 55.

CHAPTER ONE

1. James Northcote, *The Life of Sir Joshua Reynolds* (London, 1819), I, 142.

2. Hermann Voss, *Die Malerei des Barock in Rom* (Berlin, 1924), p. 655.

3. Walter Friedlander, *David to Delacroix* (Cambridge: Harvard University Press, 1952), pp. 14–15.

4. See below, pp. 47–48.

5. The artist "Grevling" defies identification. Flexner ("Benjamin West's American Neo-Classicism," p. 9) suggests that Gravelot was probably the name intended, but I

believe Gribelin, also active in England, would be more probable, if only for phonetic reasons.

6. Dunlap, I, 44.

7. William's paintings were first identified in William Sawitzky, "William Williams, First Instructor of West," *Antiques*, XXXI (1937), pp. 240–42.

8. Charles A. du Fresnoy, *The Art of Painting*, trans. John Dryden (London, 1695). It is not possible to say which essay by Richardson West was given. Whether it was *The Theory of Painting* (London, 1715) or *An Essay on the Whole Art of Criticism*, which appeared with *An Argument in Behalf of the Science of the Connoisseur* (London, 1719), Galt (I, 28) does not specify. However, it makes little difference since the ideas are essentially the same in the three books, but addressed to the painter in the first, and to the dilettante in the second and third.

9. William Sawitzky, *Matthew Pratt* (New York, 1942), p. 9.

10. Dunlap, I, 115.

11. Sawitzky ("The American Work of Benjamin West," *PMHB*, LXII [1938], pp. 433–62) presents a detailed study of the influence these artists had on West's early portraiture.

12. John H. Morgan, *Early American Painters* (New York, 1921), p. 48.

13. Sawitzky, "The American Work of Benjamin West," pp. 437–38.

14. Galt, I, 35–37. The picture was previously published in Francis Jordan, Jr., *The Life of William Henry* (Lancaster, Pa., 1910), opposite p. 30. Flexner ("Benjamin West's American Neo-Classicism," pp. 20–21) illustrates it and compares it with West's source, the frontispiece of Charles Rollin, *Ancient History* (London, 1738), IV.

15. Galt, I, 102.

16. Adolf Michaelis, *A Century of Archaeological Discoveries*, trans. B. Kahnweiler (New York, 1908), pp. 6–7.

17. Galt, I, 118.

18. Louis Hautecœur (*Rome et la Renaissance de l'Antiquité à la Fin du XVIIIe Siècle* [Paris, 1912], p. 147) mentions Winckelmann's praise for Gavin Hamilton's pictures of the *Iliad* painted in 1762–65. One of these, reproduced by Hautecœur, reveals that Hamilton probably influenced West and certainly influenced J. L. David.

19. Winckelmann was preparing publications on Herculaneum and Paestum from 1758 to 1764. *Sendschreiben von den herculanischen Entdeckungen* and *Anmerkungen über die Baukunst der Alten* both appeared in 1762. *Nachricht von den neuesten herculanischen Entdeckungen* followed in 1764, which year also saw the production of the famous *Geschichte der Kunst des Alterthums*.

20. The wide appeal of Winckelmann's ideas is evidenced by the many editions of his *Geschichte*: Dresden, 1764; Vienna, 1776; Milan, 1779; Rome, 1783; Paris, 1803.

21. The quotations from Winckelmann's *Gedanken* are taken from the translation by Henry Fuseli titled *Reflections on the Painting and Sculpture of the Greeks* (London, 1765); this from page 2.

22. *Ibid.*, p. 30.

23. *Ibid.*, p. 30.

24. Translated from J. J. Winckelmann, *Œuvres Complètes* (Paris, 1803), I, 484.

25. Joseph Farington, *The Farington Diary*, ed. James Greig (London, 1922–28), I (1795), 126. Batoni's fluent style may be studied in Hermann Voss, *Die Malerei des Barock in Rom* (Berlin, 1924), pp. 406–17.

26. J. J. Winckelmann, *Reflections*, pp. 52–55. Winckelmann wrote this before seeing the frescoes from Pompeii and Herculaneum, but these had little influence in the eighteenth century (see p. 23). What was to be seen in Rome is reproduced in George Turnbull, *A Treatise on Ancient Painting* (London, 1740), in which the plates are more curious than inspiring.

27. Anton R. Mengs, *The Works of Anthony Raphael Mengs*, trans. J. N. D'Azara (London, 1796), p. 78. The quotation is from Mengs's *Gedanken über die Schönheit und den Geschmack in der Malerei*, first published 1761.

28. Bolognese eclecticism is discussed by Nickolaus Pevsner (*Academies of Art* [Cambridge University, 1940], pp. 75–79) and in Voss, pp. 481–83. Denis Mahon (*Studies in Seicento Art and Theory* [London, 1947], pp. 195–229) casts doubt upon the eclectic theory being held by the Carracci and their school, but the proof of it for the present writer is contained in the pictures by these artists.

29. Domenichino's picture was praised by West, Galt (II, 172). West's "Raising of Lazarus" (Pl. 7) was probably based upon it. Joshua Reynolds (*The Literary Works of Sir Joshua Reynolds*, ed. Edmund Malone [London, 1819], I, 39, Discourse II) mentions Ludovico Carracci's "Transfiguration" as vividly remembered. Galt (II, 171) contains West's opinion: it "embraced nearly all the points of art."

30. *Ibid.*, I, 122. The wording of this advice is by West's biographer, John Galt, who received it many years after the event from West, but its sense is so entirely in keeping with Mengs's attitude that it is probably trustworthy. All of Mengs's idols are mentioned, except Raphael, whose name was almost too obvious to include. The special attention directed to the Bolognese school is a reminder of Mengs's own affinity with it.

31. *Ibid.*, 126; also Farington, *Diary*, V (1808), 46–47.

32. Galt, I, 142. West did most of his study in Rome after returning from the other Italian cities. He painted a "Cimon and Iphigenia" and an "Angelica and Medoro" to pass muster before Rome's critics. It has been suggested in the Philadelphia Museum catalogue, *Benjamin West, 1738–1820* (Philadelphia, 1938), p. 21, that the "Angelica and Medoro" now owned by Rutgers University (Pl. 16) might reproduce the composi-

tion which won West applause in Rome. This does not seem probable, because, as Professor Helmut von Erffa told me, the title of the Rutgers picture will have to be changed to "Rinaldo and Armida," which it surely illustrates. For this reason I have adopted the corrected title in discussing the picture later in the text.

33. The portrait "The Countess of Northampton and her Daughter," now in the Minneapolis Institute of Arts, was painted by West when he was in Venice. See the Institute's *Bulletin*, XXXIV (1945), No. 27, pp. 95–101.

34. The original by Tiepolo (or a close follower) is reproduced in Pompeo G. Molmenti, *G. B. Tiepolo* (Milan, 1909), p. 174. West's early "Last Supper," formerly in the Ehrich Galleries, New York, is also a copy; see Molmenti, opposite p. 250. I am informed of another copy by West reproducing Guercino's "Christ Taken Prisoner," recently in the possession of Mr. Julius Weitzner, New York.

35. Galt, II, 5. The Wilton House collection was very notable, containing all of Mazarine's, Richlieu's, and many of Arundel's antiques. See Richard Cowdry, *A Description of the . . . Curiosities at . . . Wilton* (London, 1751).

36. West's brief retirement was due to factious bickering within the Royal Academy. For a few months, 1805–6, James Wyatt, the royal architect, was president. See J. E. Hodgson and F. A. Eaton, *The Royal Academy and its Members* (London and New York, 1905), p. 193.

37. Farington (*Diary*, VII [1813], 180) cites attacks on West for his poor English, and Lord Lonsdale's defense, "Criticisms upon Him were upon defficiencies which a school Boy might notice & remark upon."

38. *Ibid.*, III (1804), 36.

39. See the listing under Christie, James, in the Bibliography. These catalogues of West's collections are available in the Frick Art Reference Library, New York.

40. Michaelis, *A Century of Archaeological Discoveries*, pp. 8 and 18. Herculaneum was excavated in 1711 and again between 1738 and 1766. Pompeii, discovered in 1748, was not excavated until after 1766. There was very little that might be seen of the Herculaneum finds to draw a student such as West away from Rome in 1760–63.

41. Hautecœur, *Rome et la Renaissance*, pp. 81–83, lists the descriptions and plates of Pompeii and Herculaneum published in the second half of the eighteenth century. Only the illustrations produced by the Accademia Ercolanese di Archeologia, such as *Le Pitture Antiche d'Ercolano* (Naples, 1757–79) were worth serious attention, the others having been drawn from memory. For complete early publication of these sites see Friedrich Furchheim, *Bibliographia di Pompei, Ercolano e Stabia* (Naples, 1891).

42. Giovanni P. Bellori's attitude is characteristic of the adulation extended to the classical tradition. It is expressed in his *Le Vite de' Pittori, Scultori ed Architetti Moderni* (Rome, 1672). He emphasized Raphael, Annibale Carracci, and Poussin as the most

distinguished exponents of the idealizing style, and included comments on Caravaggio as representing its antithesis. This criticism still prevailed in West's day when Caravaggio was generally ignored. Though it is difficult for a modern mind to find an entire lack of idealism in Caravaggio, and to grasp the distinctions Bellori makes, it is essential to do so if the esthetics of West's period are to be sympathetically approached.

43. Adolf Michaelis, *Ancient Marbles in Great Britain*, trans. C. A. M. Fennell (Cambridge University, 1882) contains a detailed catalogue of all the notable English collections of ancient sculpture, with an account of how the collections were formed.

44. West's praise of the Elgin marbles is given in *The Elgin Marbles from the Temple of Minerva at Athens*, published by J. Taylor (London, 1816), pp. 58–60.

45. Horace Walpole, *Aedes Walpoliana* (London, 1767, first published 1747), pp. vi–vii. For the earliest plates after statues found in Rome one may consult Thomas Ashby, "Antiquae Statue Urbis Romae," *Papers of the British School at Rome*, IX (1920), 107–58. This is a study of the many books of engravings based upon Joannes B. Cavalleriis' three volumes from the late sixteenth century. Probably still popular in West's day was Pietro-S. Bartoli, *Admiranda Romanarum Antiquitatum* (Rome, 1693), G. G. Bottari, *Del Museo Capitolino* (Rome, 1745–82), and Bartolomeo Cavaceppi, *Raccolta d'Antiche Statue* (Rome, 1768–72). Also current were Bernard de Montfaucon, *Antiquity Explained, and Represented in Sculptures*, trans. David Humphreys (London, 1721–22), Comte de Caylus, *Recueil d'Antiquités* (Paris, 1752–67), and J. J. Winckelmann, *Monumenti Antichi Inediti* (Rome, 1767; Paris, 1802).

46. Richard Dalton published the first satisfactory drawings of the Parthenon and Erechtheum in *A Series of Engravings* (London, 1751–52) and *Antiquities and Views* (London, 1749 and 1791). The Dilettanti Society furthered the investigations of James Stuart and Nicolas Revett, producing *The Antiquities of Athens, Measured and Delineated* (London, 1762–1830). The Dilettanti also promoted *Antiquities of Ionia* (London, 1769, 1797, etc.). One should not forget the publication of the Hamilton vases by Hancarville (Pierre F. Hugues), *Antiquités . . . du Cabinet de Mr. Hamilton* (Naples, 1766, 1767).

47. Fréart de Chambray, *The Idea of the Perfection of Painting*, translated by John Evelyn (London, 1668). Pierre Monier, *The History of Painting, Architecture, Sculpture and Graving* (London, 1699). Charles Rollin, *Ancient History* (London, 1738). George Turnbull, *A Treatise on Ancient Painting* (London, 1740). J. J. Winckelmann, *Reflections . . . and Instructions for the Connoisseur* (London, 1765). Only the most influential treatises prior to the eighteenth century are included in this and the following notes. For a complete listing of English art theory books from the previous century, see Henry and Margaret Ogden, "A Bibliography of Seventeenth-Century Writings on the Pictorial Arts in English," *Art Bulletin*, XXIX (1947), 196–201. For a brief discussion of

this material, see Luigi Salerno, "Seventeenth-Century English Literature on Painting," *Journal of the Warburg and Courtauld Institutes*, XIV (1951), 234–58.

48. Francis Junius, *The Art of Painting* (London, 1638). Parts of Giovanni P. Bellori, *The Idea of the Painter, the Sculptor and the Architect*, translated by John Dryden and quoted in his Introduction to Charles A. du Fresnoy, *The Art of Painting* (London, 1695), which also supported the creation of an art drawn from nature, but as idealistic as classical art. Also Ludovico Dolce, *Aretin: a Dialogue on Painting*, trans. W. Brown (London, 1770); Jonathan Richardson, *The Theory of Painting* (London, 1715) and other essays listed in note 8 to Chapter I; Joshua Reynolds, *Discourses*, ed. G. Malone (London 1797–98).

49. Jo. Paul Lomatius (Giovanni P. Lomazzo), *A Tracte Containing the Arts of Curious Paintinge, Carvinge, and Buildinge*, trans. Richard Haydock (Oxford, 1598). Lomazzo's later essay, *Idea del Tempio della Pittura* (Bologna, 1590) stressed the aim of ideal beauty, but certainly the earlier treatise (Milan, 1584), which Haydock translated, emphasized expression. Even proportion, Lomazzo's key to beauty, was made subservient to expressive ends. See *A Tracte*, Book I, p. 37 ff. Also presenting the chief aim of art as expression were Charles Le Brun, *Conference on Expression of the Passions*, trans. John Smith (London, 1701); André Félibien, *The Tent of Darius Explain'd*, trans. Col. Parsons (London, 1703); Benjamin Ralph, *The School of Raphael; or the Student's Guide to Expression in Historical Painting* (London, 1759); Anthony A. Cooper, third Earl of Shaftesbury, *Notion of the Historical Draught or Tablature of the Judgment of Hercules* (London, 1713). Shaftesbury was less directly concerned with the expression of passions than was Le Brun and others, but his insistence on the meaningful arrangement of figures and all details, and his concern with the moment of a story most pregnant with meaning, ally his *Notion* with the expressive school of classicists.

50. The *Abrégé* (Paris, 1699) was translated in Richard Graham, *Essay towards an English School of Painters* (London, 1706). The *Balance* (Paris, 1709) was included in Roger de Piles, *The Principles of Painting*, translated "by a Painter" (London, 1743).

51. William Hayley, *An Essay on Painting* (London, 1771). Martin A. Shee, *Elements of Art* (London, 1809). Mention should also be made of two useful painters' handbooks: William Salmon, *Polygraphice* (5th ed.; London, 1685), includes alchemist's secrets and a chapter of home remedies. It is the source for J. Potts, pub., *The Art of Drawing and Painting in Water-colours*, a new ed. with *The Art of Drawing in Perspective* (Dublin, 1763). A more copious handbook was offered by the Dutch Gerard de Lairesse, *The Art of Painting in All Its Branches*, translated by J. F. Fritsch (London, 1778).

CHAPTER TWO

1. West's first Discourse was published in London in 1793. This and four others are summarized and quoted in Galt, II, 83–176.

2. Du Fresnoy, p. 13.

3. *Ibid.*, p. 9. "We love what we understand; we desire what we love; we pursue the Enjoyment of those things which we desire. . . ." Thus, enjoyment was sought in understanding; reason gave pleasure.

4. *Ibid.*, pp. 11–13.

5. See Walter J. Bate, *Criticism: The Major Texts* (New York, 1952), p. 5, for a discussion of the several meanings of imitation; also Rensselaer W. Lee, "*Ut Pictura Poesis:* The Humanistic Theory of Painting," *Art Bulletin*, XXII (1940), pp. 203–10.

6. Bate, *Criticism*, p. 6.

7. Man's moral nature was understood to be an "instinct" which was part of the logical functioning of the mind, not opposed to reason. See Walter J. Bate, *From Classic to Romantic* (Cambridge, Mass., 1949), pp. 2 ff.

8. Du Fresnoy, p. 5, recommends subjects "which by their Nobleness, or by some remarkable accident, have deserv'd to be consecrated to Eternity. . . ."

9. Dunlap, I, 92–93.

10. Du Fresnoy, p. 7.

11. Aristotle *Poetics* xv. 11 (Loeb ed., 1946, p. 57). This is freely translated in Bellori, *Le Vite de' Pittori* (Rome, 1672), p. 8. See Elizabeth G. Holt (*Literary Sources of Art History* [Princeton, N.J., 1947], p. 325) for translation of Bellori quotation.

12. See the discussion by de Piles in his notes to du Fresnoy, *Art of Painting*, p. 92. West told the Zeuxis story, Galt, II, 99.

Another way ideal beauty might be determined was demonstrated by Phidias in his "Zeus" and "Athena" in which he imitated an idea of perfect beauty formed in his mind (Cicero *Orator* ii. 9, Loeb ed., 1942, p. 311). The method might be interpreted as imitation of an idea innate in the mind, a Platonic, or Neo-Platonic Idea, but there is no indication that this idea formed in the mind was not formed instead by selections from experience, as Aristotle would have contended. Lomazzo and Bellori both drew beauty Neo-Platonically from God, but Bellori followed this with the practical suggestion that artists select the beauties of external nature, and thereafter Aristotelian imitation dominated esthetic theory. See Holt, pp. 267 and 320 ff. for pertinent passages in Lomazzo and Bellori. See Lee, "*Ut Pictura Poesis*," pp. 203–10 for an elaboration of this discussion.

13. A theory which is correlative to the artist's need to select nature's beauties was

the idea that rules were necessary to govern taste. There had to be rules because without them one might not happen upon what was most beautiful. Cf. du Fresnoy, p. 11.

14. Du Fresnoy (pp. 126–30) gives de Piles' notes on proportion. He concludes by recommending Book I of Lomazzo's *Tratto dell' Arte della Pittura* (Milan, 1584). For complete discussion of human proportions, see Erwin Panofsky, *Albrecht Dürer* (Princeton, N.J., 1945), I, 260–70.

15. Galt, II, 110.

16. Du Fresnoy, p. 7. On p. 92, de Piles' note explains that beauty for the ancient works was selected from nature according to physicians' opinions of good health, "since Beauty and Health ordinarily follow each other."

17. Du Fresnoy, pp. 75–77. The "moderns" afforded the chief examples of excellence in coloring, which was acknowledged "soothing and pleasing," though it was "a deceiving Beauty" (p. 37). West's color theory and practice is discussed below in the Appendix.

18. Winckelmann, *Reflections*, pp. 256–57.

19. Reynolds, *Works*, II, 99.

20. Winckelmann, *Reflections*, p. 19. Cf. Reynolds, *Works*, III, 97: ". . . to paint particulars is not to paint nature, it is only to paint circumstances."

21. A comparison of an early letter by West to Copley, 1773, with West's Discourse of 1811 will show how consistently West maintained the academic theory. The letter is in *The Letters and Papers of John Singleton Copley and Henry Pelham* (Cambridge, Mass., 1914), pp. 194–97. The Discourse of 1811 is summarized in Galt, II, 147–76.

22. Bellori, *Le Vite*, p. 8, "Now the *Idea* of this beauty is not single, but rather its forms are diverse, strong and magnanimous, pleasant and delicate, of every age and sex." Translated in Holt, p. 325.

23. Galt, II, 107.

24. Aristotle *Poetics* xv. 4 (*ed. cit.*, 1946, p. 55).

25. Leonardo da Vinci, *A Treatise on Painting*, trans. J. F. Rigaud (London, 1901), p. 63. Cf. Xenophon *Memorabilia* III. x. 1–6 (Loeb ed., 1938, pp. 231–35) for Socrates' statement of the same idea. Classical psychology was unchanged until the nineteenth century.

26. Du Fresnoy, p. 19. The problem of raising the expression of emotions to ideal forms is evaded by du Fresnoy. Lomazzo had made an effort to formulate the passions in the third book of the *Trattato*, 1584. He ordered the emotions according to the four natures of man, the four elements, and the dictates of the planets. He also suggested that colors might convey emotions: black indicates "sorrow and grief," red implies "courage and stomacke" in war, etc.

27. Charles Le Brun, *Traité des Passions* (Paris, 1698). Charles Mitchell has called

attention to West's use of Le Brun's *Passions* in "Benjamin West's *Death of General Wolfe*," *Journal of the Warburg and Courtauld Institutes*, VII (1944), 31.

28. Benjamin Ralph, *The School of Raphael* (London, 1759).

29. Galt, II, 125.

30. *Ibid.*, pp. 130–31.

31. *Ibid.*, p. 163.

32. Du Fresnoy, pp. 15 and 31.

33. *Ibid.*, p. 33.

34. Galt, II, 48. Dependent upon the painter's need for factual accuracy was the theory that the artist must be a learned man. See the list of books de Piles considered indispensable for the artist, listed in du Fresnoy, pp. 111–15. For the similar opinion of West, see *Discourse* (London, 1793), p. 31.

35. Du Fresnoy, p. 15.

36. *Ibid.*, p. 57. The moral aims of classicizing art demanded that the artist himself be virtuous, "since every Painter paints himself in his own Works" (p. 65). Cf. West, *Discourse*, pp. 31–32.

37. De Piles' note in du Fresnoy, p. 165. Arthur O. Lovejoy (*The Great Chain of Being* [Cambridge, Mass., 1936], pp. 183 ff.) shows the persistence of this idea of a social hierarchy in the eighteenth century. Each degree of social distinction was necessary for the total order of the universe.

38. Du Fresnoy, pp. 7 and 11.

39. West, *Discourse*, p. 8.

40. Xenophon *Memorabilia* II. i. 21–34 (*ed. cit.*, pp. 95–103).

41. Shaftesbury, *Judgment of Hercules* (1714 ed.), pp. 22–23. In a letter from Naples of 1712 Shaftesbury tells that he is having Paolo de Matteis paint a picture to illustrate his ideas. The letter is printed in the 1773 edition of the *Characteristics*, III, 394–410. The print of the picture first appeared in the 1713 edition of the *Characteristics*. West would have known the print and evidently tried "improving" Matteis' Baroque taste.

42. Herodotus I. 128–30 (Loeb ed., 1946, pp. 167–71). Galt (II, 50–51 and 207) lists this picture as "Cyrus Receiving the King of Armenia and Family Prisoners." In the same year, 1772, West painted another theme of heroic munificence for the king, "The Wife of Arminius Brought Captive before Germanicus," which is in Kensington Palace, London. Galt lists this as "Germanicus Receiving Sagastis and his Daughter Prisoners." It illustrates Tacitus *Annals* I. lvii–lviii (Loeb ed., 1943, pp. 339–43).

43. Galt (II, 25–26) cites the source for this story as Livy, but it is told in Horace *Odes* iii. 5 (Loeb ed., 1939, pp. 195–99). Another tale of patriotic determination is seen in "Hannibal Taking the Oath," Kensington Palace, illustrating Livy XXI. 4 (Loeb ed. 1929, p. 5).

44. Tacitus *Annals* III. 1 (*ed. cit.*, 1943, p. 523).

45. Epaminondas' death is related in Diodorus Siculus xv. 87 (Loeb ed., 1952, p. 197). One cannot tell West's source for the Bayard story since it would appear in any French history book. Bayard (*ca.* 1473–1524) was one of the most popular French heroes; his life was published by Jacques Joffrey, Paris, 1527.

46. Homer *Iliad* vi. 389–493 (Loeb ed., 1937, pp. 291–97).

47. Plutarch *Coriolanus* xxxiv–xxxvi (Loeb ed., 1916, pp. 203–19). Also Shakespeare, *Coriolanus*, Act V, scene 3.

48. Homer *Iliad* xiv. 153–225 (Loeb ed., 1939, pp. 79–83). It seems very probable that the "Townley Venus" was the source for West's figure types in this painting.

49. Ovid *Metamorphoses* x. 708–39 (Loeb ed., 1939, pp. 115–17).

50. Arthur O. Lovejoy, "Monboddo and Rousseau," *Essays in the History of Ideas* (Baltimore, 1948), pp. 38–61.

51. James Burnett, Lord Monboddo, *Antient Metaphysics* (Edinburgh, 1779–99), *passim*.

52. William Smith, *An Historical Account of the Expedition against the Ohio Indians in the Year 1764* (Dublin, 1769).

53. The picture is undated, but was probably painted 1775–76 when both Johnson and Brant were in London. This date seems more probable than *ca.* 1779, which is suggested in the National Gallery of Art, *Preliminary Catalogue of Paintings and Sculpture* (Washington, 1941), p. 213, because at the earlier date Johnson had just been confirmed in his appointment as superintendent of Indian Affairs, and a portrait with Indian attributes would have been in order. See Carolyn T. Foreman, *Indians Abroad* (Norman: University of Oklahoma, 1943), p. 94.

54. It is inviting to believe that the plate illustrated here was West's source, but it was first published in 1767 in Rome, one year later than West's painting of the theme. He might have had access to the plates of Wincklemann's *Monumens inédit* before their publication, but it is just as probable that he sketched an Orestes sarcophagus himself.

55. Jean Locquin (*La Peinture d'Histoire en France de 1747 à 1785* [Paris, 1912], p. 154) mentions the "Antinoos" and unspecified priestesses of Diana as prototypes for West's picture.

56. Galt (II, 5) tells that West went to Hampton Court soon after arriving in London and saw Raphael's Cartoons. West owned a set of engravings after them, partially colored by Thornhill. See Christie, *Catalogue of the truly Capital Collection . . .* (London, 1820), p. 15.

57. Winckelmann, *Reflections*, p. 32.

58. See Heinrich Wölfflin, *Principles of Art History*, trans. M. D. Hottinger (New York, n.d.), pp. 73–100, and for another approach to the same distinction between

Renaissance and Baroque painting, Grose Evans, "The Baroque Harmony of Space and Form," *Gazette des Beaux-Arts*, per. 6, XXXIX (1952), pp. 27–36.

59. There is an unfinished version of this famous picture now owned by Knoedler, New York City, to whom I am indebted for the following information. It was listed as No. 80 in the George Robins Sale "of the late Benjamin West's pictures," June 20 and 22, 1829, and is described as a duplicate. It appears to be by West's hand, and has hung in the Derby Mechanics' Institute since about 1844.

60. Walpole's marginal notes from his Royal Academy exhibition catalogues are printed in Algernon Graves, *The Royal Academy of Arts* (London, 1905–6). In Vol. VIII, p. 213, Graves quotes this comment on West's style, "His first manner was in changeable colours like Baroccio." On page 212 Walpole's remark on "Penn's Treaty" is given, "This picture, which contains many figures, was painted in three weeks, has good drawing and great merit. . . . The colouring, like all his pictures in his second manner, is heavy, brickish, and void of clearness." It will be noted that Walpole distinguished two manners within West's early style on the basis of bright or dark colors, but in view of West's total development, this distinction by coloring alone does not seem to merit a division into another stylistic phase in the present study.

CHAPTER THREE

1. Edmund Burke, *A Philosophical Enquiry into the Origin of our Ideas of the Sublime and Beautiful* (London, 1757).

2. For the consequences of this shift in interest to particular instead of ideal nature, see Arthur O. Lovejoy, " 'Nature' as Aesthetic Norm," *Essays in the History of Ideas* (Baltimore, 1948), pp. 69–77. For the influence of empiricism on English writers on taste, see Bate, *From Classic to Romantic*, pp. 55–58, and 94 ff.

3. In Part III of his essay Burke rejected the usually accepted classicizing explanations of beauty as due to proportions, fitness for function, and perfection, both physical and spiritual. Page references in the following notes are to *The Works of the Right Honorable Edmund Burke* (3rd ed.; Boston: Little, 1869).

4. Burke, Pt. III, secs. 12–18 (*Works*, I, 191–97).

5. *Ibid.*, sec. 27 (pp. 205–7).

6. Burke cites many examples for the various senses to show how pleasure and pain result from the exercise of perception. One instance will serve to illustrate his theory. In speaking of looking at very large objects, he says, "the eye must traverse the vast space of such bodies with great quickness, and consequently the fine nerves and muscles destined to the motion of that part must be very much strained; and their great sen-

sibility must make them highly affected by this straining." *Ibid.*, Pt. IV, sec. 9 (p. 218).

7. Aristotle *On Memory and Reminiscence* 2. 415b. For the eighteenth-century use see Bate, *From Classic to Romantic*, p. 96, and Martin Kallich, "The Association of Ideas and Critical Theory: Hobbes, Locke, and Addison," *ELH*, XXI (1945), 290–315.

8. Burke, Pt. IV, sec. 2 (*Works*, I, 210).

9. *Ibid.*, Pt. I, sec. 13 (p. 117).

10. *Ibid.*, Pt. IV, sec. 6 (p. 215). Earlier (Pt. I, sec. 4 [p. 107]), Burke defined delight as "the feeling which results from the ceasing or diminution of pain," as a state not opposed to pain or pleasure, but arbitrating between these extremes, and giving positive satisfaction.

11. *Ibid.*, Pt. IV, sec. 6 (p. 215).

12. *Ibid.*, sec. 7 (p. 216).

13. *Ibid.*, Introduction (p. 94).

14. See Samuel H. Monk, *The Sublime* (New York, 1935).

15. Particularly by Richard Payne Knight; see pp. 83–84.

16. Burke, Pt. II, sec. 4 cont. (*Works*, I, 156).

17. *Ibid.*, Pt. V, sec. 7 (p. 259). On *Obscurity* as a fundamental source of the Sublime; see Pt. II, secs. 3, 4, 4 cont. (pp. 132–38).

18. *The Exhibition of the Royal Academy* (London, 1798), p. 5, No. 76. The picture was painted for William Beckford and hung in Fonthill Abbey.

19. Burke, Pt. II, sec. 3 (*Works*, I, 133).

20. The only example of a subject from Milton painted by West which I have encountered is listed in Graves, *The Royal Academy of Arts*, VIII, 219. Here under the date 1809 is entered, "Milton's Messiah from the sixth book of Paradise Lost. . . ." However, the same subject is listed in *West's New Gallery* (London, 1828), p. 31, with a quotation from Revelation 1:7. West's dependence upon Milton's description of Death is attested in the description of "Death on the Pale Horse" in *West's New Gallery*, p. 19: "Mr. West was of opinion that, to delineate a physical form, which in its moral impression would approximate to that of the visionary Death of Milton, it was necessary to endow it, if possible, with the appearance of superhuman strength and energy. . . ."

21. Burke, Pt. II, sec. 8 (*Works*, I, 148).

22. Burke (Pt. II, sec. 5 [*Works*, I, 139]) offers this parallel: "An ox is a creature of vast strength; but he is an innocent creature. . . . A bull is strong too; but his strength is of another kind; often very destructive . . . the idea of a bull is therefore great, and it has frequently a place in sublime descriptions, and elevating comparisons."

23. *Ibid.* (p. 140). Burke has compressed here the description of the horse given in the Book of Job 39: 19–24.

24. *Description of Mr. West's Picture of Death on the Pale Horse* (n.p., n.d.), anony-

mous pamphlet in the Library of Congress, p. 3. Also printed in *West's New Gallery*, p. 18.

25. Two letters from West to Lord Elgin, thanking him for permission to copy the Parthenon marbles are printed as an Appendix in William R. Hamilton, *Memorandum on the Subject of the Earl of Elgin's Pursuits in Greece* (London, 1811), pp. 47–56.

26. The date *ca.* 1787 has been suggested for the first painted version (Pl. 43) in the Philadelphia Museum catalogue, *Benjamin West* (Philadelphia, 1938), pp. 39–40. This dating is based upon the statement made in 1817 by William Carey in his *Critical Description and Analytical Review of "Death on the Pale Horse"* (London, 1817), p. 115, "The subject has been meditated upon for more than thirty years. . . . In the first sketch on paper, and in the small painting. . . ." Here these references are assumed to refer to the two small oil paintings, but probably Carey intended the words "sketch on paper" to indicate the drawing of 1783. Thus it seems reasonable to suppose the first oil sketch dates also *ca.* 1783.

27. Kimball, "Benjamin West au Salon de 1802," p. 403.

28. Monk, pages 77–79, discusses the widespread tendency of the eighteenth century to interpret the Scriptures esthetically, citing passages from Shaftesbury, Johnson, Robert Lowth, Coleridge, and others wherein the sublimity of the Bible is mentioned.

29. Galt, II, 193–98. A list of these subjects is given by Galt on pages 209–11 compiled from West's account rendered to the king, and telling which pictures were completed and which were only sketched. It is impossible to identify extant pictures for this commission with certainty, for the works were dispersed from Windsor Castle at an unknown time, and the only basis of relationship now would be similarity of title.

30. Another picture equally notable for all the sinister trappings of the Gothic novel, and of even earlier date, 1772, is the "Cave of Despair," reproduced in Henry Moses, *The Gallery of Pictures Painted by Benjamin West* (n.p., 1811). It illustrates Spenser's *Faerie Queene*, Book I, canto xi.

31. These are preserved in the Royal Collections. The following titles and dates have been supplied by the Lord Chamberlain's Office, St. James's Palace, London:

"The Battle of Crécy," 1788. (Formerly called "Edward III Forcing the Passage of the River Somme in France," Galt, II, 214).

"The Black Prince Receiving King John after the Battle of Poitiers," 1788.

"The Consecration of the Statutes of the Order of the Garter," 1787.

"Edward III Embracing the Black Prince after the Battle of Crécy," n.d.

"Edward III Entertaining his Prisoners after the Surrender of Calais," 1788. (Formerly called "Edward III Crowning Ribemont at Calais," Galt, II, 214).

"Queen Philippa at the Battle of Neville's Cross," 1789.

"Queen Philippa Interceding for the Burgesses of Calais," 1789.

"St. George Destroying the Dragon," n.d.

32. See Elizabeth W. Manwaring, *Italian Landscape in Eighteenth Century England* (New York, 1925) and H. F. Clark, *The English Landscape Garden* (London, 1948).

33. Frank Simpson, "Dutch Painting in England before 1760," *Burlington Magazine*, XCV (1953), 39–42. West himself had a large collection of Dutch and Flemish pictures. See Christie, *Catalogue of the truly Capital Collection . . .* (London, 1820).

34. William Gilpin, *An Essay on Prints* (London, 1768), p. 2.

35. William Gilpin, *Observations, Relative Chiefly to Picturesque Beauty . . . Particularly the Mountains and Lakes of Cumberland and Westmoreland* (London, 1786), I, 81–132 and II, 11. A good summary of Gilpin's theory of picturesqueness is given in William D. Templeman, *The Life and Work of William Gilpin* (Urbana, Ill., 1939), pp. 131–46.

36. Gilpin, *Mountains and Lakes*, I, 121–22.

37. *Ibid.*, I, 228, cites Burke's opinions.

38. Uvedale Price, *Essays on the Picturesque* (London, 1798), I, 106–7 and *An Essay on the Picturesque* (London, 1796).

39. For Knight's depreciations of Price's notions, see Richard Payne Knight, *An Analytical Inquiry into the Principles of Taste* (London, 1805), *passim*. An excellent discussion of the controversy is in Christopher Hussey, *The Picturesque* (London and New York, 1927), pp. 68–82.

40. Leslie Stephen in *DNB*, s.v. "Gilpin, William."

41. Farington, *Diary*, IV (1807), 211–12. West's interest in landscape again appeared in his enthusiasm for the panorama (a picture mounted continuously around the walls of a display room) invented by Robert Barker, and first shown in the Haymarket Theatre in 1789. West allowed Barker to quote him as having said it was the greatest improvement in painting yet discovered! See William T. Whitley, *Artists . . . in England, 1700–1799* (London and Boston, 1928), II, 107.

42. Burke, Pt. II, sec. 1 (*Works*, I, 130).

43. Leigh Hunt, *Autobiography* (London, 1949), p. 88.

44. Homer *Iliad* xix. 12–27 (Loeb ed., 1939, pp. 337–39). The appropriateness of dramatic gesture and facial expression is, of course, determined by personal taste, and the paragraph above is based on the writer's feeling. West's dramatic figures must be seen in the light of his contemporaries' expectations, which may be guessed in part from the popularity of David Garrick's acting. In comparison with Garrick's "fireworks," West's figures do not seem overly melodramatic. See Margaret Barton, *Garrick* (New York, 1949).

45. John Flaxman, *Lectures on Sculpture* (London, 1865), p. 25. A painting by Charles Bestland shows West presiding at the Royal Academy with the "Laocoon" cast towering above him. See Hodgson and Eaton, *Royal Academy*, opposite p. 166.

46. Christie, *Catalogue of the Remaining and Reserved Part . . .* (London, 1824), p. 36.

47. West mentioned the "Laocoon" himself in his Discourses, Galt, II, 126, 152. Winckelmann expressed enthusiasm for it in *Reflections*, p. 30 ff., and Lessing's famous essay, appearing in 1766, attested the eighteenth-century respect of it.

48. Homer *Iliad* viii. 130–44 (Loeb ed., 1937, p. 349).

49. Burke, Pt. II, sec. 4 cont. (*Works*, I, 136).

50. *Ibid.*, sec. 14 (p. 156).

51. *Ibid.*, sec. 16 (p. 158).

52. *Ibid.*, Pt. III, sec. 27 (pp. 205–6).

CHAPTER FOUR

1. Richard Payne Knight, *An Analytical Inquiry into the Principles of Taste* (London, 1805). References in these notes will be made to the fourth edition of 1808.

2. *Ibid.*, p. 336.

3. *Ibid.*, p. 338.

4. *Ibid.*, p. 362.

5. *Ibid.*, p. 338.

6. *Ibid.*, p. 333.

7. *Ibid.*, pp. 339–40.

8. *Ibid.*, p. 358.

9. *Ibid.*, p. 361.

10. Farington, *Diary*, VII (1813), 192.

11. Knight, p. 311.

12. Farington, *Diary*, IV (1807), 151.

13. *Ibid.*, IV (1807), 150.

14. The elaborate symbolism in West's sketch for a monument to Nelson, of which this picture was to be the central part, is given in Graves, *The Royal Academy of Arts*, VIII, 218–19. The sketch is at Cooper Union, New York City (Pl. 67).

15. Knight, p. 351.

16. This subject is not found in Procopius' account of Belisarius; it seems to have been a fiction, traceable back to the tenth century. It was popularized chiefly in J. F. Marmontel's *Belisaire* (Paris, 1767). See *Encyclopædia Britannica* (1945) s.v. "Belisarius." Though West's painting was made before the publication of Knight's *Principles*

of Taste, 1805, West's acquaintance with Knight may explain its close relationship with Knight's ideas on pity.

17. J. Taylor, pub., *Elgin Marbles* (London, 1816), p. 59. West wrote: "Whether in studying them [the Elgin marbles], I have added any celebrity to the productions of my pencil, I leave the Select Committee to determine, on viewing my two Works, subsequent to those studies, viz. Christ in the Temple, and Christ Rejected. . . ."

18. Farington, *Diary*, v (1808), 46.

19. Taylor, pub., *Elgin Marbles*, p. 59.

20. *Ibid.*, p. 59. But he did prefer Elgin's sculptures above the Phigaleian marbles, Knight's bronzes, or Townley's statues.

21. Galt, II, 150–52.

22. West may have seen this picture by Poussin because in 1741 it entered the Radnor Collection, which he visited, *ibid.*, p. 5, or he could have known a print of it. Prints were made by J. Audran, S. Baudet, and S. Gantrel according to Otto Grautoff, *Nicolas Poussin* (Munich and Leipzig, 1941), II, 148, No. 88.

23. Farington, *Diary*, VII (1813), 143.

24. Knight, p. 339.

25. *Ibid.*, p. 348.

26. A. D. M'Quin, *A Description of the Picture "Christ Rejected by the Jews"* (Philadelphia, 1830), front cover.

27. See Walter J. Bate, "The Sympathetic Imagination in Eighteenth-Century English Criticism," *ELH*, XII (1945), 144–64.

28. A description of "Christ Rejected" is given in *West's New Gallery* (London, 1828) which, on pp. 8–9, omits the reference in the Bible to Caiaphas, but associates the picture with a prophecy from Isaiah, chapter 23, with the Pilate and Barabbas episode in Matthew, chapter 27, and with the mocking of Christ in Luke, chapter 23 and John, chapter 19. This would seem to strengthen the idea that West intended spectators to associate the picture rather freely with various biblical passages.

29. The analogies established here between "Christ Rejected" and Crucifixion iconography in no way negate the probability that Poussin's picture, cited above as a compositional parallel, also served to influence his composition. West's method was to merge several adaptations into one work.

30. West owned a framed colored print of Rubens' "Descent from the Cross"; see Christie, *Catalogue of the truly Capital Collection* . . . (London, 1820), p. 7. He used the Deposition iconography for most of his "death of a hero" scenes: Plates 5, 26, 27, 64, and 66.

31. Charles Mitchell ("Benjamin West's Death of General Wolfe," *Journal of the Warburg and Courtauld Institutes*, VII [1944], 31) publishes apt sources for West's

"Death of General Wolfe," in Van Dyck's "Deposition," Munich; Rembrandt's "Deposition," London, as well as faces from Le Brun's *Conference* (London, 1701). I cannot subscribe to the very weak analogies suggested in Oskar Hagen, *The Birth of the American Tradition in Art* (London and New York, 1940), p. 115.

32. A similar gesture by St. John is discussed and traced ultimately to Greek and Roman sculpture in Dorothy C. Shorr, "The Mourning Virgin and St. John," *Art Bulletin*, XXII (1940), 61–69.

33. Christie, *Catalogue of the truly Capital Collection . . .* (London, 1820), p. 5.

34. This probability is heightened by the drawing for "Agrippina Mourning" in the Pennsylvania Historical Society. In this the child behind the woman's leg is a boy instead of a girl as in the painting, so that the similarity to St. John playing with the Christ child at the Madonna's knee is obvious. The background figures are absent in the drawing, thus the familiar Madonna grouping is immediately apparent (Pl. 24).

35. It is reproduced in André Félibien, *The Tent of Darius Explain'd*, trans. Col. Parsons (London, 1703), frontispiece. West also sometimes used the heroic deathbed scene as in "The Meeting of Lear with Cordelia," Huntington Library, San Marino, California, and in the sketch for this in the Folger Library, Washington, D.C. A print after West's "Stratonice," reproduced in Hagen, Fig. 100, is another instance. Hagen claims this is modeled after J.-L. David's prize winning picture done a year before West's, but surely the relationship between them can be explained by the fact that both artists drew upon the traditional treatment of the deathbed scene, as it can be seen in Poussin's "Death of Germanicus," Minneapolis Institute of Art, Minneapolis, Minn.

36. West's sources were related to the battle scene tradition—the "Amazon Sarcophagus," which shows a battle, and Rubens' "Lion Hunt," which owes a great deal to the study of Leonardo's "Battle of Anghiari."

APPENDIX

1. Farington, *Diary*, II (1803), 171.

2. *Ibid.*, VIII (1817), 154.

3. Cf. *ibid.*, VIII (1816), 105. West demonstrated his points in Thornhill's copies of the Cartoons, then hanging in the Royal Academy. West applied his theory in practice occasionally, achieving a "rainbow" disposition of colors by using the three primary hues broadly and distinctly throughout a composition. His "Appeal to Coriolanus" (Pl. 23) is an example, for it has a golden atmospheric setting and a liberal use of red, blue, and yellow in the costumes. The analogy of a rainbow is perhaps not too far-fetched, since the effect is exuberant and pleasing.

4. It is helpful in understanding this passage to recall the sequence of colors in Newton's spectrum: Violet, Indigo, Blue, Green, Yellow, Orange, Red.

5. Galt, II, 113–14. The concluding idea concerning reflected color is carried on from seventeenth-century theory, cf. du Fresnoy, p. 47.

6. In West's painting, the use of color he described here can best be seen in his sketches, where his touches of paint are distinct. "The Meeting of Lear with Cordelia" in the Folger Library, Washington, D.C., shows the warm tones reserved for highlighted areas, while the shades and shadows are painted in relatively cooler hues.

7. Farington, *Diary*, V (1808), 11–12.

8. He used a tenebrist method of coloring far less successfully than his Rainbow and Venetian styles of coloring. This called for broad shadowed areas of "brown sauce" to give chiaroscuro effects. West was not a strong enough draftsman to succeed in this manner, and his contrasting areas of light are inaccurately modeled to achieve the tenebrist's solid, emerging forms; "Death on the Pale Horse," 1817, suffers from this shortcoming.

9. Farington, *Diary*, IV (1807), 115–16.

10. *Ibid.*, IV (1807), 150.

11. Dunlap (I, 106) quotes Sir Martin Archer Shee's opinion that West was not a good colorist. This view was widely held in West's own day.

12. See Paul Signac, *D'Eugène Delacroix au Néo-Impressionisme* (Paris, 1939). Joachim Gasquet, *Cézanne* (Paris, 1921), contains conversations in which Cézanne described his efforts to grasp the relation of form and color simultaneously. West's theory was at least a rationalist's attempt in this direction. M. E. Chevreul and H. L. F. von Helmholtz were the scientists especially known to painters through their publications.

BIBLIOGRAPHY

——————— ✳ ———————

BOOKS

Accademia Ercolanese di Archeologia. *Le Pitture Antiche d'Ercolano*. Five vols. Naples, 1757–59.

Addison, Agnes E. *Romanticism and the Gothic Revival*. Philadelphia, 1938.

Aglionby, William. *Painting Illustrated in Three Dialogues, containing some choice Observations upon the Art*. London, 1686.

Alison, Archibald. *Essays on the Nature and Principles of Taste*. Edinburgh and London, 1790.

Baker, C. H. Collins. *British Painting*. Boston, 1933.

Barbault, J. *Les plus beaux Monuments de Rome ancienne*. Rome, 1761.

Barker, Virgil. *American Painting*. New York, 1950.

Barlow, Joel. *The Vision of Columbus*. Baltimore, 1814.

Barry, James. *The Works of James Barry*. London, 1809.

Bartoli, Petro-Santi. *Admiranda Romanarum Antiquitatum*. Rome, 1693.

Bartoli, Pietre-Sancte. *Recueil de Peintres Antiques*. Paris, 1757.

Barton, Margaret. *Garrick*. New York, 1949.

Bate, Walter J. *Criticism: The Major Texts*. New York, 1952.

———. *From Classic to Romantic: Premises of Taste in Eighteenth-Century England*. Cambridge, 1949.

Bellori, Giovanni P. *Le Vite de' Pittori, Scultori, ed Architetti Moderni*. Rome, 1672.

Bieber, Margarete. *Laocoon: The Influence of the Group since its Rediscovery*. New York, 1942.

Blunt, Anthony. *Artistic Theory in Italy*. Oxford, 1940.

129

———— and Whinney, Margaret. *The Nation's Pictures*. London, 1950.

Bottari, G. G. *Del Museo Capitolino*. Four vols. Rome, 1745–82.

Boydell, John. *A Collection of Prints Engraved after the most Capital Paintings in England*. Two vols. London, 1769, 1772.

————. *A Collection of Prints from Pictures Painted for the Purpose of Illustrating the Dramatic Works of Shakespeare by the Artists of Great Britain*. Two vols. London, 1803.

Burke, Edmund. *A Philosophical Enquiry into the Origin of our Ideas of the Sublime and Beautiful* in *The Works of the Right Honorable Edmund Burke*. Third edition. Boston: Little, 1869. I, pp. 67–262. First published 1756; first complete edition 1757.

Burke, Joseph T. A. "A Biographical and Critical Study of Benjamin West, 1738–1792, with a Supplemental Chapter on his Circle." Unpublished M.A. thesis, Yale University, 1937.

Byron, George Gordon, Lord. *The Complete Works of Lord Byron.*, ed. J. W. Lake. Paris, 1825.

Carey, William. *Critical Description and Analytical Review of "Death on the Pale Horse."* London, 1817.

Carritt, E. F. *Philosophies of Beauty*. New York, London, and Toronto, 1931.

Carson, Hampton L. *Life and Works of Benjamin West: An Address Delivered before the Historical Society of Pennsylvania*. Philadelphia, 1921.

Cavaceppi, Bartolomeo. *Raccolta d' Antiche Statue, Busti, Teste Cognite ed altre Sculture Antiche Scelte*. Three vols. Rome, 1768, 1769, and 1772.

Caylus, Comte de. *Recueil d'Antiquités Égyptiennes, Etrusques, et Romaines*. Seven vols. Paris, 1752–67.

————. *Recueil de Trois Cent Têtes*. Paris, 1775.

Chamberlain, Arthur B. *George Romney*. New York, 1910.

Chambray, Fréart de. *The Idea of the Perfection of Painting*. London, 1668.

Christie, James. *A Catalogue of the truly Capital Collection of Italian, French, Flemish, and Dutch Pictures which were selected . . . by Benjamin West, Esq., P.R.A., Deceased. . . .* London, June 23, 1820.

————. *A Catalogue of the Remaining and Reserved Part of the very Valuable Collection of Italian, French, Flemish, and Dutch Pictures of Benjamin West, Esq., Deceased. . . .* London, May 28, 1824.

————. *Catalogue of the First Part of the Superb Collection of Prints and Drawings Formed by the late Benjamin West, Esq., R.A.* London, June 9, 1820.

————. *Catalogue of the Last Part of the Superb Collection of Drawings, Prints, and Books of Prints, Formed by the late Benjamin West, Esq., P.R.A.* London, July 1, 1820.

BIBLIOGRAPHY

Christie, Mason, and Woods. *Catalogue of the Collection of Pictures, Drawings, and Sketches by Benjamin West, P.R.A.* London, March 18–19, 1898.

Clark, H. F. *The English Landscape Garden.* London, 1948.

Clark, Kenneth. *The Gothic Revival.* London, 1950.

Cowdry, Richard. *A Description of the Pictures, Statues, Busto's, Basso-Relievo's, and other Curiosities at the Earl of Pembroke's House at Wilton.* London, 1751.

Dalton, Richard. *Antiquities and Views in Greece and Egypt.* Two vols. London, 1749 and 1791.

———. *A Series of Engravings Representing Views . . . in Sicily, Greece, Asia Minor, and Egypt.* Two vols. London, 1751–52.

De Piles, Roger. *Abrégé de la Vie des Peintres.* Paris, 1699.

———. *The Principles of Painting.* London, 1743.

Description of Mr. West's Picture of Death on the Pale Horse. Anonymous pamphlet in the Library of Congress. No place, no date.

Dictionary of National Biography, ed. Leslie Stephen. London, 1890.

Dolce, Ludovico. *Aretin: A Dialogue on Painting.* Translated by W. Brown. London, 1770.

Du Bos, Jean B. *Critical Reflections on Poetry, Painting and Music.* Translated by Thomas Nugent. Three vols. London, 1748.

Du Fresnoy, Charles A. *The Art of Painting.* Translated by John Dryden. Second ed.; London, 1716; first published 1695.

———. *The Art of Painting.* Translated by William Mason in *The Literary Works of Sir Joshua Reynolds*, ed. Edmund Malone. Volume III. London, 1819.

Dunlap, William. *A History of the Rise and Progress of the Arts of Design in the United States.* Volume I. Boston, 1918. First published 1834.

The Exhibition of the Royal Academy. Catalogues since 1769. London.

Farington, Joseph. *The Farington Diary*, ed. James Greig. Eight vols. London, 1922–28.

Faulkner, Thomas. *History and Antiquities of Kensington.* London, 1820.

Félibien, André. *The Tent of Darius Explain'd; or the Queens of Persia at the Feet of Alexander.* Translated by Col. Parsons. London, 1703.

Flaxman, John. *Compositions from the Hell, Purgatory, and Paradise of Dante Alighieri.* Engraved by Thomas Piroli. London, 1793.

———. *Illustrations to Homer.* No place, no date.

———. *Lectures on Sculpture.* London, 1865.

Flexner, James T. *America's Old Masters.* New York, 1939.

Furchheim, F. *Bibliographia di Pompei, Ercolano e Stabia.* Naples, 1891.

Fuseli, Henry. *The Life and Writings of Henry Fuseli*, ed. John Knowles. Three vols. London, 1831.

Galt, John. *The Life and Studies of Benjamin West, Esq., President of the Royal Academy of London, prior to his Arrival in England.* Philadelphia, 1816.

———. *The Life, Studies, and Works of Benjamin West, Esq., President of the Royal Academy in London, Composed from Materials Furnished by Himself.* Two vols. London, 1820.

Gasquet, Joachim. *Cézanne.* Paris, 1921.

Gilbert, Katherine E. and Kuhn, Helmut. *A History of Aesthetics.* Bloomington, Ind., 1953.

Gilpin, William. *Observations, Relative Chiefly to Picturesque Beauty, Made in the Year 1772, on Several Parts of England; particularly the Mountains, and Lakes of Cumberland and Westmoreland.* Two vols. London, 1786.

———. *Observations . . . on . . . the Coasts of Hampshire, Sussex, and Kent.* London, 1804.

———. *Observations . . . on . . . the Highlands of Scotland.* London, 1789.

———. *Observations . . . on . . . the New Forest.* London, 1790.

———. *Observations . . . on . . . the River Wye and South Wales.* London, 1782.

———. *Observations . . . on . . . Western England and The Isle of Wight.* London, 1798.

Graham, Richard. *Essay Towards an English School of Painters.* London, 1706.

Grant, Col. Maurice H. *A Chronological History of the Old English Landscape Painters.* Two vols. London, no date.

Graves, Algernon. *The Royal Academy of Arts: A Complete Dictionary of the Contributors and their Work from its Foundation in 1769 to 1904.* Volume VIII. London, 1905–6.

Hagen, Oskar. *The Birth of the American Tradition in Art.* London and New York, 1940.

Hamilton, William R. *Memorandum on the Subject of the Earl of Elgin's Pursuits in Greece.* London, 1811.

Hamilton, Sir William. *Outlines from the Figures and Compositions upon the Greek, Roman, and Etruscan Vases of the late Sir Wm. Hamilton.* Engraved by Mr. Kirk. London, 1804.

Hancarville (Pierre F. Hugues). *Antiquités Etrusques, Greques et Romaines tirées du Cabinet de Mr. Hamilton.* Four vols. Naples, 1766–67.

Hautecœur, L. *Rome et la Renaissance de l'Antiquité à la Fin du XVIIIe Siècle.* Paris, 1912.

Haydon, Benjamin R. *Correspondence and Table-talk.* Two vols. London, 1876.

Hayley, William. *An Essay on Painting in Two Epistles to Mr. Romney.* London, 1771.

Hazlitt, William. *Conversations of James Northcote, Esq., R.A.* London, 1949. First published 1830.

Highet, Gilbert. *The Classical Tradition.* London and New York, 1949.

Hodgson, John E. and Eaton, Fred A. *The Royal Academy and its Members*. London and New York, 1905.

Hogarth, William. *The Analysis of Beauty*. London, 1810. First published 1753.

Holt, Elizabeth G. *Literary Sources of Art History*. Princeton, N.J., 1947.

Howe, Percival P. *The Life of William Hazlitt*. New York, 1922.

Hunt, Leigh. *Autobiography*. London, 1949. First published 1850.

Hussey, Christopher. *The Picturesque*. London, 1927.

Jones, H. Stuart (ed.). *Select Passages from Ancient Writers Illustrative of the History of Greek Sculpture*. London and New York, 1895.

Jordan, Francis, Jr. *The Life of William Henry*. Lancaster, Pa., 1910.

Junius, Francis. *The Painting of the Ancients*. London, 1638.

Justi, Carl. *Winckelmann und seine Zeitgenossen*. Two vols. Leipzig, 1943.

Keats, John. *The Letters of John Keats*, ed. Maurice B. Forman. Two vols. Oxford, 1931.

Kitto, H. D. F. *The Greeks*. Harmondsworth, 1951.

Knight, Richard Payne. *An Analytical Inquiry into the Principles of Taste*. London, 1808. First published 1805.

Lairesse, Gerard de. *The Art of Painting in All Its Branches*, translated by J. F. Fritsch (London, 1778).

Lavater, John C. *Physiognomy*. Translated by Henry Fuseli. London, 1786.

Le Brun, Charles. *Conference on Expression of the Passions*. Translated by John Smith. London, 1701.

Le Clerc, Sebastien. *Les Vrais Principes du Dessein suivis du Caractère des Passions*. Paris, no date.

Leonardo da Vinci. *A Treatise on Painting*. Translated by J. F. Rigaud. London, 1901. First published 1877.

Le Roy, Julien D. *Les Ruines des plus Beaux Monuments de la Grece*. Paris, 1758.

Leslie, Charles R. *Memoirs of the Life of John Constable*. London, 1937.

Lester, C. Edwards. *The Artists of America*. New York, 1846.

The Letters and Papers of John Singleton Copley and Henry Pelham. ("Massachusetts Historical Society Collection," Vol. LXXI.) Cambridge, 1914.

Locquin, Jean. *La Peinture d'Histoire en France de 1747 à 1785*. Paris, 1912.

Lomazzo, Giovanni P. *Idea del Tempio della Pittura*. Bologna, 1590.

————. *A Tracte Containing the Arts of Curious Paintinge, Carvinge, and Buildinge: written first in Italian by Jo: Paul Lomatius of Milan and Englished by R. H. (Richard Haydock) student in Physik*. Oxford, 1598. Italian edition published 1584.

Longinus, Dionysius. *Dionysius Longinus on the Sublime*. Translated by William Smith. London, 1770.

Lovejoy, Arthur O. *Essays in the History of Ideas*. Baltimore, 1948.

————. *The Great Chain of Being.* Cambridge, Mass., 1936.

M'Quin, A. D. *A Description of the Picture "Christ Rejected by the Jews."* Philadelphia, 1830.

Manwaring, Elizabeth W. *Italian Landscape in Eighteenth Century England.* New York, London, and Toronto, 1925.

Maréchal, P. S. *Antiquités d'Herculanum.* Engraved by F. A. David. Twelve vols. Paris, 1780–1803.

Mengs, Anton Raphael. *The Works of Anthony Raphael Mengs.* Translated by Don Joseph Nicholas D'Azara. London, 1796.

Michaelis, Adolf. *A Century of Archaeological Discoveries.* Translated by B. Kahnweiler. New York, 1908.

————. *Ancient Marbles in Great Britain.* Translated by C. A. M. Fennell. Cambridge University, 1882.

Molmenti, Pompeo G. *G. B. Tiepolo.* Milan, 1909.

Monboddo, Lord (James Burnett). *Antient Metaphysics or the Science of Universals.* Six vols. Edinburgh, 1779–99.

Monier, Pierre. *The History of Painting, Sculpture, Architecture, Graving: And of Those who have Excell'd in Them.* Translated from French. London, 1699.

Monk, Samuel H. *The Sublime: a Study of Critical Trends in XVIII-Century England.* New York, 1935.

Montfaucon, Bernard de. *Antiquity Explained, and Represented in Sculptures.* Five vols. Translated by David Humphreys. London, 1721–22.

Morgan, John H. *Early American Painters.* ("John Divine Jones Fund Series of Histories and Memoirs," IV.) New York: The New-York Historical Society, 1921.

Morse, Edward L. (ed.). *Samuel F. B. Morse, His Letters and Journals.* Two vols. Boston, 1914.

Moses, Henry. *The Gallery of Pictures Painted by Benjamin West.* No place, 1811.

Northcote, James. *The Life of Sir Joshua Reynolds.* Two vols. London, 1819.

Patch, Thomas. *Prints after Giotto, Masaccio, Bartolommeo.* Three vols. Florence, 1770 and 1772.

Pevsner, Nickolaus. *Academies of Art.* Cambridge University, 1940.

Philadelphia Museum of Art. *Benjamin West, 1738–1820.* Catalogue. Philadelphia, 1938.

Piroli, Tommaso. *Le Antichità di Ercolano.* Six vols. Rome, 1789–1807.

Plumb, J. H. *England in the Eighteenth Century.* Harmondsworth, 1950.

Potts, J. (pub.). *The Art of Drawing and Painting in Water-colours and the Art of Drawing in Perspective.* Dublin, 1763.

Price, Uvedale. *An Essay on the Picturesque, as Compared with the Sublime and Beautiful.* London, 1796.

————. *Essays on the Picturesque.* Two vols. London, 1798.

Ralph, Benjamin. *The School of Raphael; or the Student's Guide to Expression in Historical Painting . . . and the Passions as Characterized by Raphael in the Cartoons.* London, 1759.

Redford, George. *Art Sales.* Two vols. London, 1888.

Redgrave, Richard and Samuel. *A Century of Painters of the English School.* London, 1871.

Reynell, C. and W. (pub.). *West's New Gallery, Catalogue of Pictures and Drawings by the Late Benjamin West, Esq.* London, 1828.

Reynolds, Joshua. *The Literary Works of Sir Joshua Reynolds,* ed. Edmund Malone. Three vols. London, 1819.

Richardson, Jonathan. *The Theory of Painting.* London, 1715.

————. *Two Discourses: An Essay on the Whole Art of Criticism and An Argument in Behalf of the Science of the Connoisseur.* London, 1719.

————. *The Works of Jonathan Richardson.* London, 1792. First published 1773.

Richter, Gisella M. A. *The Sculpture and Sculptors of the Greeks.* New Haven, Conn., 1950.

Roberts, William. *Memorials of Christie.* Two vols. London, 1897.

Robinson, John. *A Description of, and Critical Remarks on the Picture of "Christ Healing the Sick in the Temple."* Philadelphia, 1835.

Rollin, Charles. *Ancient History.* Volume IV. London, 1738.

Salmon, William. *Polygraphice, or the Arts of Drawing, Engraving, Etching, Limning, Painting, Washing, Varnishing, Guilding, Colouring, Dying, Beautifying and Perfuming.* Fifth ed.; London, 1685.

Sandby, William. *The History of the Royal Academy of Arts.* Two vols. London, 1862.

Sartain, John. *Description of West's Greatest Picture, "Christ Rejected."* Philadelphia, 1864.

Satchwell, R. *Scripture Costume . . . Drawn under the Supervision of Benjamin West, Esq.* London, 1819.

Sawitzky, William. *Matthew Pratt, 1734–1805.* New York, 1942.

Scriven, Edward. *Elements of Drawing in a Series of Examples Extracted from Pictures Painted by and in the Gallery of Benjamin West, Esq.* London, 1821.

Sellers, Charles. *The Artist of the Revolution: The Early Life of Charles Willson Peale.* Hebron, Pa., 1939.

Shaftesbury, Anthony A. Cooper, Third Earl of. *An Essay on Painting, being a Notion of the Historical Draught or Tablature of the Judgment of Hercules.* London, 1714.

Shee, Martin A. *Elements of Art, a Poem in Six Cantos.* London, 1809.

Signac, Paul. *D'Eugène Delacroix au Néo-Impressionisme.* Paris, 1939.

Sitwell, Sacheverell. *British Architects and Craftsmen.* London, 1945.

Smith, John T. *Nollekens and His Times.* Two vols. London, 1829.

Smith, William. *An Historical Account of the Expedition against the Ohio Indians in the Year 1764 under the Command of Henry Bouquet, Esq.* Dublin, 1769.

Society of Dilettanti. *Antiquities of Ionia.* London, 1769–1915.

————. *Specimens of Ancient Sculpture.* Two vols. London, 1809 and 1835.

————. *The Unedited Antiquities of Attica.* London, 1817.

The Spectator, ed. H. Morley. London, 1891.

Stuart, James and Revett, Nicholas. *The Antiquities of Athens, Measured and Delineated.* London, 1762–1830.

Summerson, John. *Georgian London.* New York, 1946.

Taylor, J. (pub.). *The Elgin Marbles from the Temple of Minerva at Athens.* London, 1816.

Templeman, William. *The Life and Work of William Gilpin.* Urbana, Ill., 1939.

Tischbein, William. *Collection of Engravings from Ancient Vases . . . now in the possession of Sir Wm. Hamilton.* Three vols. Naples, 1791, 1795.

Turnbull, George. *A Treatise on Ancient Painting.* London, 1740.

Vertue, George. *A Catalogue and Description of King Charles the First's Capital Collection.* London, 1757.

Voss, Hermann. *Die Malerei des Barock in Rom.* Berlin, 1924.

Walpole, Horace. *Aedes Walpoliana, or a Description of the Pictures at Houghton Hall in Norfolk.* London, 1767. First published 1747.

————. *Anecdotes of Painting in England.* Three vols. London, 1876. First completely published 1780.

Ward, James. *Conversations of James Northcote, R.A. with James Ward*, ed. Ernst Fletcher. London, 1901. First published 1830.

Weisbach, Werner. *Französischer Malerei des XVII. Jahrhunderts.* Berlin, 1932.

West, Benjamin. *A Discourse Delivered to the Students of the Royal Academy, December 10, 1792.* London, 1793.

Whitley, William T. *Art in England, 1800–1820.* New York and Cambridge University, 1928.

————. *Art in England, 1821–1837.* New York and Cambridge University, 1930.

————. *Artists and their Friends in England, 1700–1799.* Two vols. London and Boston, 1928.

Winckelmann, Johann J. *De l'Allégorie, ou Traités sur cette Matière.* Paris, 1799. First published 1766.

————. *Histoire de l'Art chez les Anciens par Winckelmann, Traduite de l'Allemand avec Notes Historiques et Critiques de Differens Auteurs.* Three vols. Paris, 1803. First published 1764.

————. *Monumens inédit de l'Antiquité*. Translated by A. F. Desodards. Three vols. Paris, 1808 and 1809. First published 1767.

————. *Reflections on the Painting and Sculpture of the Greeks, and Instructions for the Connoisseur*. Translated by Henry Fuseli. London, 1765. First published 1755.

Wornum, Ralph (ed.). *Lectures on Painting by the Royal Academicians, Barry, Opie, and Fuseli*. London, 1848.

ARTICLES

Ashby, Thomas. "Antiquae Statue urbis Romae," *Papers of the British School at Rome*, IX (1920), 107–58.

Baker, C. H. Collins. "Some Illustrations of Milton's *Paradise Lost*," *The Library*, ser. 5, III (1948), 1–21, 101–21.

Bate, Walter J. "The Sympathetic Imagination in Eighteenth-Century English Criticism," *ELH, A Journal of English Literary History*, XII (1945), 144–64.

Denvir, Bernard. "Benjamin West and the Revolution in Painting," *Antiques*, LXXI (1957), 347–49.

Erffa, Helmut von. "An Oil Sketch by Benjamin West," *Register of the Museum of Art of the University of Kansas*, No. 7 (May, 1956), pp. 1–7.

————. "King Lear by Benjamin West," *Bulletin of the Rhode Island School of Design*, XLIII (December, 1956), pp. 6–8.

————. "West's The Washing of Sheep, Genre or Portrait?" *The Art Quarterly*, XV (1952), 160–65.

Flexner, James T. "The Amazing William Williams: Painter, Author, Teacher, Musician, Stage Designer, Castaway," *Magazine of Art*, XXXVII (1944), 243–46.

————. "The American School in London," *Bulletin of the Metropolitan Museum*, VII (1948), 64–72.

————. "Benjamin West's American Neo-Classicism," *The New-York Historical Society Quarterly*, XXXVI (1952), 5–41.

Hazlitt, William. "Mr. West's Picture of *Christ Rejected*," *The Champion: a London Weekly Journal*, June 25, 1814, p. 205. Also issues of September 10, 1814, p. 294, and October 1, 1814, p. 318.

Kallich, Martin. "The Association of Ideas and Critical Theory: Hobbes, Locke, and Addison," *ELH, A Journal of English Literary History*, XXI (1945), 290–315.

Kimball, S. Fiske. "Benjamin West au Salon de 1802," *Gazette des Beaux-Arts*, ser. 6, VII (1932), 403–10.

Lee, Rensselaer W. "*Ut Pictura Poesis*: The Humanistic Theory of Painting," *Art*

Bulletin, XXII (1940), 197–269.

Locquin, Jean. "La Part de l'Influence Anglaise dans l'Orientation Néo-Classique de la Peinture Française entre 1750 et 1780," *Actes du Congrès d'Histoire de l'Art*, II (1921), 391–402.

Mayor, A. Hayatt. "Early American Painters in England," *American Philosophical Society Proceedings*, LXXXVII (1943), 105–9.

Mitchell, Charles. "Benjamin West's *Death of General Wolfe*," *Journal of the Warburg and Courtauld Institutes*, VII (1944), 20–33.

Munby, A. N. L. "Letters of British Artists of the XVIIIth and XIXth Centuries, Part III," *Connoisseur*, CXIX (1947), 29–33.

Neumeyer, Alfred. "The Early Historical Paintings of Benjamin West," *Burlington Magazine*, LXXIII (1938), 162–65.

Ogden, Henry V. S. and Margaret. "A Bibliography of Seventeenth-Century Writings on the Pictorial Arts in English," *Art Bulletin*, XXIX (1947), 196–201.

Olguin, Manuel. "The Theory of Ideal Beauty in Arteaga and Winckelmann," *The Journal of Aesthetics and Art Criticism*, VIII (1949), 12–33.

Pleasants, J. Hall. "George William West, a Baltimore Student of Benjamin West," *Art in America*, XXXVII (1949), 7–47.

Salerno, Luigi. "Seventeenth-Century English Literature on Painting," *Journal of the Warburg and Courtauld Institutes*, XIV (1951), 234–58.

Sawitzky, William. "The American Work of Benjamin West," *Pennsylvania Magazine of History and Biography*, LXII (1938), 433–62.

————. "William Williams, First Instructor of Benjamin West," *Antiques*, XXXI (1937), 240–42.

Semon, Kurt M. "His Sketches Reveal the Scope of Benjamin West's Work as an Artist," *American Collector*, XIV (1945), 6–7 and 19.

Shorr, Dorothy C. "The Mourning Virgin and St. John," *Art Bulletin*, XXII (1940), 61–69.

Simpson, Frank. "Dutch Painting in England before 1760," *Burlington Magazine*, XCV (1953), 39–42.

Todd, Ruthven. "Benjamin West vs. the History Picture," *Magazine of Art*, XLI (1948), 301–5.

Wind, Edgar. "Penny, West, and *The Death of General Wolfe*," *Journal of the Warburg and Courtauld Institutes*, X (1947), 159–62.

INDEX

———————— ✳ ————————

139

LANDSCAPE, 70–73, Pls. 54, 55

Lanfranco, Giovanni, 52

"Laocoon": Winckelmann's opinion of, 15–16, 122n47; effect on West, 77; mentioned, 94, 122n45

Lawrence, Sir Thomas: praises West, 108n5; mentioned, 103

Le Brun, Charles: on the passions, 36, 37; his *Tent of Darius*, 101; mentioned, 27, 124n31

Leonardo da Vinci: on emotions, 36; West on, 37; his "Battle of Anghiari," 124n36

Lessing, Gotthold, 122n47

Livy, 116n43

Lomazzo, Giovanni: on beauty, 114n12; on emotions, 115n26; mentioned, 27

London, England: West in, 3, 21–22, 40; Royal Academy of, 3, 22, 40, 45, 77; painting and sculpture collections of, 21, 24–25

Longford Castle, 21

Longinus on the Sublime, 60, 83

Lorrain, Claude. *See* Claude Lorrain

Lowth, Robert, 120n28

M'QUIN, A. D., 97, Pl. 71

Matteis, Paolo de: "Judgment of Hercules," 42

Mead, Dr. Richard, 24

"Meeting of Lear with Cordelia," 124n35, 125n6

Mengs, Anton Raphael: his "Parnassus," 9, 16–17, 20, Pl. 14; life and art, 16–19; advice to West, 18–19; influence on West, 20, 42; mentioned, 14

Michelangelo, 23, 33

Middleton, Conyers, 24

Milton, John: description of Death, 61–62

"Milton's Messiah," 119n20

"Mrs. West and her Son Raphael," 101, Pl. 73

Monboddo, James Burnett, Lord, 45–46

Monier, Pierre, 27

Moses, Henry, 120n30

NATURE, ideal. *See* Classical art theory

Neoclassicism, 4, 40–42, 102. *See also* Classicism; Classical art theory; David; Mengs; Stately Mode; Winckelmann

New York, N.Y., 12

Noble Savage, 45–46

"OMNIA Vincit Amor," 77, 79–80, Pl. 60

Ovid: his *Metamorphoses*, 117n49, Pl. 31

Oxford, England, 21

PARMA, Italy, 19, 53

Parmesan painting, 33, 53, 54

Pathetic Style: definition of, 5–6, 83; theory of, 83–86, 87; West's pictures in, 88–95, 97; mentioned, 57, 64. *See also* Composition; Knight, Richard Payne

Peale, Charles Willson, 31

Pembroke, Thomas Herbert, eighth Earl of, 24–25

"Penn's Treaty with the Indians," 46, 51, 54, 118n60, Pl. 35

Petworth Castle, 25

Phidias, 27, 94, 114n12. *See also* Elgin marbles

Philadelphia, Pa.: painters of, 11–12

Picturesque, 70–73

Pitt, William, 43

Platonic Idea, 114n12

Plutarch: his *Coriolanus*, 44, Pl. 23

Pompeii, Italy, 23

Poussin, Nicolas: composition of, 50–51; influence on West, 88; his "Worship of the Golden Calf," 94–95, 123n29, Pl. 72; his "Death of Germanicus," 124n35; mentioned 111n42

Pratt, Mathew, 11–12

Price, Uvedale, 72

"Pylades and Orestes," 9–10, 47–48, 51, Pl. 9

"QUEEN Philippa at the Battle of Neville's Cross," 120n31

"Queen Philippa Interceding for the Burgesses of Calais," 69, 121n31, Pl. 50

"RAISING of Lazarus": painting of 1780, 7, Pl. 8; painting of 1776, 110n29, Pl. 7

Ralph, Benjamin, 27

Raphael: influence on West, 10, 48, 50–52; influence on Mengs, 17; Cartoons as expressive models, 36–37; his "Christ Giving the Keys to Peter," 48; his "Sacrifice at Lystra," 48, 52, Pl. 11; his "School of Athens," 50; West turns from, 74, 78; his "Madonna del Cardelino," 101; his "Madonna della Sedia," 101; Thornhill's copies of, 124n3; mentioned, 16, 23, 33, 34, 95, 103, 111n42

ILLUSTRATIONS

1   *Benjamin West.* Agrippina Landing at Brundisium with the Ashes of Germanicus, 1766.
Courtesy of the Yale University Art Gallery, New Haven, Conn.

2   Relief from
the ARA PACIS.

Published in P. S. Bartolo,
*Admiranda Romanarum
Antiquitatum,* 1693, Pl. 15.

3   *Benjamin West.* The Angel of the Lord Announcing the Resurrection to the Marys
at the Sepulchre, 1805.

In the Brooklyn Museum Collection, Brooklyn, N.Y.

4   *Benjamin West*. Christ Healing the Sick in the Temple, 1811.

Pennsylvania Hospital, Philadelphia, Pa.

5   *Benjamin West*. The Death of General Wolfe (second version), *ca*. 1769.

Kensington Palace, London. Copyright Reserved.

6 *Benjamin West*. Saul and the Witch of Endor, 1777.

7   *Benjamin West*. The Raising of Lazarus (study), 1776; retouched 1814

Swarthmore College, Swarthmore, Pa.

8   *Benjamin West*. The Raising of Lazarus, 1780.

Collection of the Wadsworth Atheneum, Hartford, Conn.; Gift of J. Pierpont Morgan.

9

Benjamin West. Pylades and Orestes, 1766.
Reproduced by courtesy of the Trustees of the Tate Gallery, London.

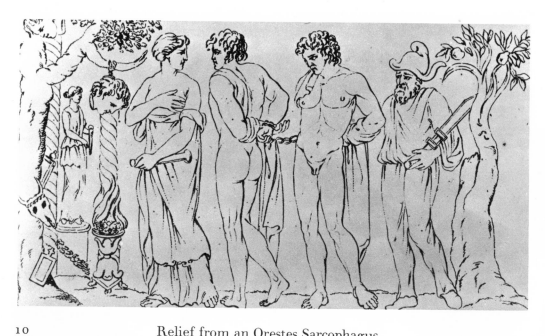

10   Relief from an Orestes Sarcophagus.

Published in Winckelmann, *Monumens Inedits*, III, Plate 149.

11   *Raphael*. The Sacrifice at Lystra.

Victoria & Albert Museum, London: Crown Copyright.

Benjamin West. Elizabeth Peel, *ca.* 1756.
Courtesy of The Pennsylvania Academy of the Fine Arts, Philadelphia, Pa.

13   *Benjamin West.* The Death of Socrates, *ca.* 1756.

Mrs. Thomas H. A. Stites, Boulton, Nazareth, Pa. Photograph courtesy of the Frick Art Reference Library, New York, N.Y.

14 *Anton Raphael Mengs.* Parnassus, 1760–61.

Villa Albani, Rome.

15 *Domenichino.* The Hunt of Diana, *ca.* 1617.

Borghese Gallery, Rome. Alinari photo.

16   *Benjamin West*. Rinaldo and Armida, 1766; retouched 1790.

Rutgers University, New Brunswick, N.J.

17   *Giovanni Tiepolo*. The Agony in the Garden.
              Mainfränkisches Museum, Würzburg.

18   *Benjamin West*. Christ on the Mount of Olives, 1760–63.

The Elgin Academy Art Gallery, Elgin, Ill.

19   *Benjamin West*. The Departure of Regulus, *ca.* 1767.

20   *Benjamin West*. The Choice of Hercules, 1764.

Victoria & Albert Museum, London: Crown Copyright.

21   The Vatican Meleager.

Vatican Museums and Galleries,
Vatican City.

22   *Benjamin West.* Cyrus Liberating the Family of Astyges, 1772.
Buckingham Palace, London. Copyright Reserved.

23   *Benjamin West*. The Appeal to Coriolanus, 1770–80.

The Folger Shakespeare Library, Washington, D.C.

24   *Benjamin West*. Study for "Agrippina and her Children Mourning
over the Ashes of Germanicus," 1771.

From the collection of the Historical Society of Pennsylvania, Philadelphia, Pa.

25   *Benjamin West*. Agrippina and her Children Mourning over the Ashes of Germanicus, 1773.
The John and Mable Ringling Museum of Art, Sarasota, Fla.

26   *Benjamin West*. The Death of the Chevalier Bayard, 1771.

27   *Benjamin West*. The Death of Epaminondas, 1771.

Kensington Palace, London. Copyright Reserved.

28   *Benjamin West*. Hector Parting with his Wife and Child at the Scæn Gate, 1771.

Courtesy of the New-York Historical Society, New York, N.Y.

29   *Benjamin West.* Juno Receiving the Cestus from Venus, 1771.

Formerly Robert C. Vose Galleries, Boston, Mass.

30   *Benjamin West*. Una and the Lion, 1772.

Collection of the Wadsworth Atheneum, Hartford, Conn.

31   *Benjamin West*. Venus Lamenting the Death of Adonis, 1772.

Carnegie Institute, Pittsburgh, Pa.

32   *Benjamin West*. Paintings on the Dome of the Royal Academy

Air, Water, Earth, and Fire, 1770–80.
Royal Academy of Arts, London.

33 *Benjamin West.*
Colonel Guy Johnson, 1775-76.

National Gallery of Art, Washington, D.C.
(Mellon Collection)

34 *After Benjamin West.*

Published in William Smith's
Expedition against the Ohio Indians, 1769.
New York Public Library, New York, N.Y.

35   *Benjamin West*. Penn's Treaty with the Indians, 1772.

Courtesy of The Pennsylvania Academy of the Fine Arts, Philadelphia, Pa.

36 *Benjamin West.*
Peter Denying Christ,
ca. 1780.

37 *Ludovico Carracci.*
Christ and the Woman
of Canaan, *ca.* 1595.

Brera Gallery, Milan
(Ediz. Istituto Italiano
d'Arti Grafische, Bergamo).

Benjamin West. Hagar and Ishmael, 1776; retouched 1803.

Courtesy of the Metropolitan Museum of Art, New York, N.Y.

39   *Benjamin West*. The Ascension of Our Saviour, *ca.* 1780.

40   *Ludovico Carracci*. The Transfiguration.

Bologna Gallery. (D. Anderson photo.)

41   *Benjamin West*. The Archangel Gabriel, 1798.

Courtesy of Mrs. Linden T. Harris, Drexel Hill, Pa.

42 *Benjamin West*. Death on the Pale Horse (drawing), 1783; retouched 1803.
Royal Academy of Arts, London.

43 *Benjamin West*. Death on the Pale Horse (first oil sketch), *ca.* 1783.
Courtesy of the Philadelphia Museum of Art, Philadelphia, Pa.

44   *Benjamin West*. Death on the Pale Horse (second oil sketch), 1802.

Courtesy of the Philadelphia Museum of Art, Philadelphia, Pa.

45   *Benjamin West*. Death on the Pale Horse (final version), 1817.

Courtesy of the Pennsylvania Academy of the Fine Arts, Philadelphia, Pa.

46

Peter Paul Rubens. The Lion Hunt.

Engraving by S. Bolswert.

47

Drawing of a relief: Battle of the Amazons.

Windsor Castle.

48   *Benjamin West*. Left and right panels of "The Conversion of Saint Paul":
Paul Persecuting the Christians and Paul's Restoration to Sight by Ananias, 1786.

Smith College Museum of Art, Northampton, Mass.

49   *Benjamin West*. The Conversion of Saint Paul, 1786.

Smith College Museum of Art, Northampton, Mass.

50   *Benjamin West*. Queen Philippa Interceding for the Burgesses of Calais, 1788.
The Detroit Institute of Arts, Detroit, Mich.

51   *Benjamin West*. King Edward III Entertaining his Prisoners after the Battle of Calais, 1788.

Benjamin West. The Battle of Crécy, 1788.
Buckingham Palace, London. Crown Copyright Reserved.

53   *Benjamin West*. Thetis Bringing the Armor to Achilles, 1806.

Art Museum of the New Britain Institute, New Britain, Conn.

54   *Benjamin West*. Woodcutters in Windsor Great Park, 1795.

The John Herron Art Museum, Indianapolis, Ind.

55   *Benjamin West*. View from the Terrace at Windsor, *ca.* 1785.

Reproduced by courtesy of the Trustees of the Tate Gallery, London.

56   *Benjamin West*. The Destruction of the Beast and the False Prophet, 1804.
The Minneapolis Institute of Arts, Minneapolis, Minn.

57   *Benjamin West.* King Lear, *ca.* 1789.

Courtesy of the Boston Athenaeum through the Museum of Fine Arts, Boston, Mass.

58   *Benjamin West*. Diomed and his Horses Stopped by the Lightning of Jupiter, 1793.

Formerly J. Leger and Sons. Photo courtesy of the Frick Art Reference Library, New York, N.Y.

59   *Peter Paul Rubens.* The Defeat of Sennacherib.

Engraving by P. Soutman.

60

Benjamin West. Omnia Vincit Amor, 1811.

Courtesy of the Metropolitan Museum of Art, New York, N.Y.

61   *Benjamin West*. Saint Paul Shaking off the Viper, 1787.

62   *Benjamin West*. Elijah Convincing the False Prophets of Baol, 1798.

Amherst College, Amherst, Mass.

63   *Benjamin West.* The Conversion of Saint Paul, 1812.

Saint Paul's Church, Richmond, Va.

64   *Benjamin West*. The Death of Lord Nelson, 1811.

Walker Art Gallery, Liverpool.

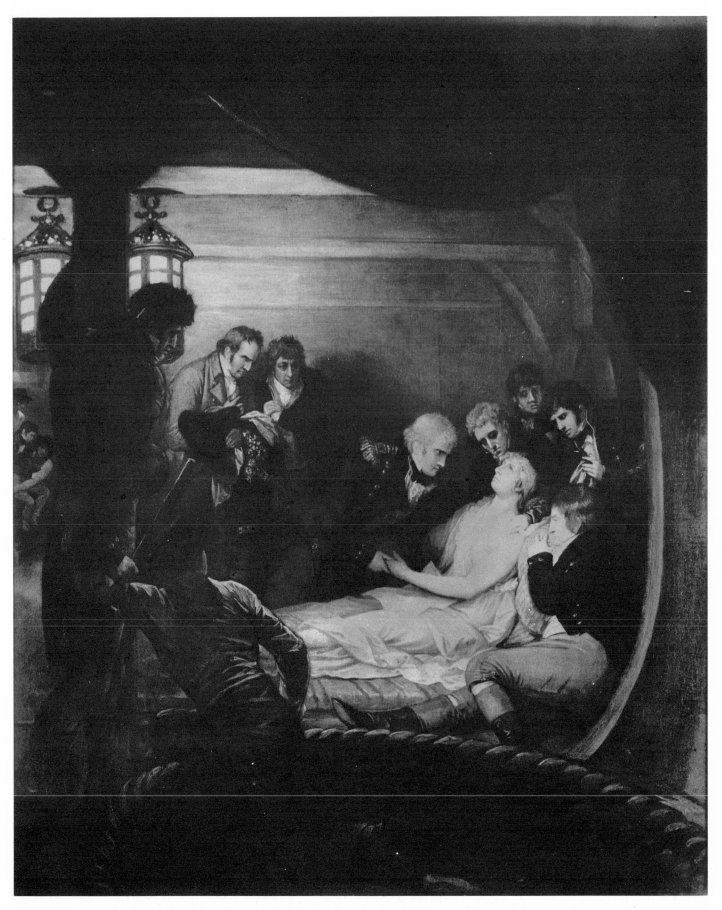

Benjamin West. The Death of Nelson, 1808.

National Maritime Museum, Greenwich.

66   *Benjamin West*. The Apotheosis of Nelson, 1807.

National Maritime Museum, Greenwich.

CXXII.
BATTLES.

THE ROYAL ASSENT TO EARL NELSONS ANNVITY
BILL OF FIVE THOVSAND POVNDS · ONE HVNDRED
AND TWENTY THOVSAND FOR THE PVRCHASE OF A SPLENDID
DOMAIN FOR THE FAMILY·

NELSON

67   *Benjamin West*. Project for a Monument: The Apotheosis of Nelson, *ca*. 1807.

Benjamin West. Belisarius and the Boy, 1802.

The Detroit Institute of Arts, Detroit, Mich.

69   *Benjamin West*. Cupid and Psyche, 1808.

In the Collection of The Corcoran Gallery of Art, Washington, D.C.

70   *Benjamin West*. Christ Rejected by the Jews, 1814.

Courtesy of the Pennsylvania Academy of the Fine Arts, Philadelphia, Pa.

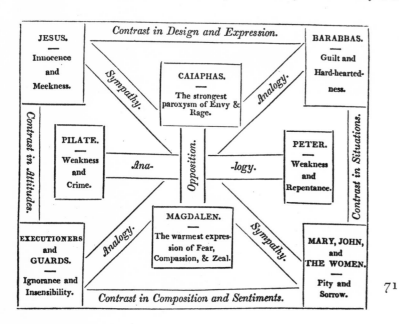

71   *A. D. M'Quin*. Diagram of
"Christ Rejected by the Jews," 1830.

72   *Nicolas Poussin*. The Worship of the Golden Calf.

Reproduced by courtesy of the Trustees, the National Gallery, London.

73   *Benjamin West*. Mrs. West and her Son Raphael, *ca.* 1770.
The Cleveland Museum of Art, Charles W. Harkness Collection, Cleveland, Ohio.